The Philosophy Book

The Philosophy Book

An A–Z of Philosophers and Ideas in Sophie's World

Otto A. Böhmer

Translated by Anthony Vivis

Phoenix House
LONDON

First published in Great Britain in 1999
by Phoenix House
a division of Orion Books Ltd,
Orion House, 5 Upper St Martin's Lane
London WC2H 9EA

Originally published in German under the title *Sofies Lexikon*,
copyright © 1997 by Carl Hanser Verlag,
München Wien, Germany

Copyright © Otto A. Böhmer 1997
Translation copyright © Anthony Vivis 1999

A catalogue record for this book is
available from the British Library

Typeset at The Spartan Press Ltd,
Lymington, Hants

Printed in Great Britain by
Butler & Tanner Ltd, Frome and London

ISBN 1 86159 149 7

Albertus Magnus

....

Albertus Magnus, whose real name was Albert von Bollstädt, lived from 1193 to 1280, and was a Dominican, theologian and philosopher. He taught in Padua, Paris, Cologne and Würzburg. For two years, from 1260 to 1261, he served as the Bishop of Regensburg.

People admired this man's great learning, but also felt a little sceptical towards it, sensing that this kind of knowledge might be rather too soft on people. Albertus Magnus believed that the philosophy of *Aristotle* could be reconciled with Christian faith. Because of his position, however, he had to acknowledge that the latter had a prior claim to higher truth.

'Aquinas had a famous philosophy teacher called Albert the Great . . .'
SW 156

Alexander the Great

The King of Macedonia (356–323 BC) was less famous as a philosopher than as a general. In this role, he subjugated the Persian Empire, among his other conquests, and helped Greek culture and civilization achieve even greater influence.

Alexander owed his first contact with philosophy to *Aristotle*. From 343 BC onwards, *Aristotle* tried his luck as a tutor at the Macedonian court, though he felt he had little success in this role.

Later, Alexander is said to have had a memorable dialogue with the philosopher *Diogenes*, who made it clear to the general that even one of the greatest figures in the world could get things wrong.

'One day while he was sitting beside his barrel enjoying the sun, he was visited by Alexander the Great . . .'
SW 109–10

Analytic philosophy

In analytic philosophy, which brings together several strands of twentieth-century thought, restraint is everything. The movement distanced itself from nineteenth-century metaphysical systems, concentrating instead on what can be done and said.

This form of philosophy examines how statements and concepts are actually used, as well as the – not always immediately obvious – context in which they can be applied. As a result, philosophy can take on only relatively minor issues, and is obliged to forgo highly revealing visions. Instead, it deals in solid definitions, whose usefulness is determined by such processes as the precise examination – in other words, analysis – of language, especially 'ordinary language'.

This approach can be traced back to Ludwig Wittgenstein (1889–1951). Having found the widest currency among the analytic movement, it has been extended in many different forms. As well as this form, there are several other variants based more directly on formally logical or categorical arguments. Seen against the background of traditional philosophy's mania for making assertions, these variants seem remarkably obsessed with detail.

'Another {such current} is the so-called *analytical philosophy* or *logical empiricism*, with roots reaching back to Hume and British empiricism . . .'
SW 383

4

Anaxagoras

Anaxagoras (500–428 BC) came from the Greek colony of Clazomenae in Asia Minor. He moved to Athens, and worked as a philosopher for many years almost without any competition. In old age, he was accused of sacrilege, though this did not lead to any judgement against him. After this, he withdrew to Lampsacus where, shortly before he died, he is said to have founded one of the earliest schools of philosophy.

Of Anaxagoras's writings, only a few fragments of his main work, *Peri Physeos* (*On Nature*) have survived. These tell us that a philosopher accepts many different 'spermata' (seeds) as the basic building blocks of life. These seeds are divisible and, according to which characteristic predominates, they determine what is particular and variable about things.

Anaxagoras was one of the first thinkers who ventured to imagine a non-material power responsible for creating and controlling cosmic forces. He called this power 'nous' (mind or spirit).

'Anaxagoras . . . was another philosopher who could not agree that one particular basic substance – water, for instance – might be transformed into everything we see in the natural world . . .'
SW 33

Anaximander

Like his colleagues, *Thales* and *Anaximenes*, Anaximander (*c.*610–545 BC) came from the Ionian town of Miletus, on the coast of Asia Minor. He is said to have had many interests and to have drawn the first map of the world. Anaximander laid the foundations of a philosophy of life with a very modern ring.

At its centre is what he called the 'boundless', which is imperishable and immortal, meaning it can also be described as the 'divine'. According to Anaximander, this impressive, though in the final analysis incomprehensible, substance is threaded through the whole cosmos, which exists alongside myriad other worlds.

Anaximander also originated a theory of development that was later to have an influence on biological science as well as philosophy. His theory was that the influence of the sun's rays created all living things out of a kind of primeval slime. In other words, the first stirrings of human life probably began where land meets water.

'The next philosopher we hear of is *Anaximander*, who also lived in Miletus . . .'
SW 29

Anaximenes

Anaximenes (*c.*546–*c.*525 BC) left no writings, and so we have only accounts from chroniclers to go on. All these mention his preference for the element of air. He believed that air fills the whole cosmos like an everlasting intake of breath.

Along with the elements of fire, water and earth, all of which were less important to him, Anaximenes thought that air made up observable reality as we know it. Finally, he believed that air is what supports the earth – which he called a 'table-like entity' – and holds it in space.

'A third philosopher from Miletus was *Anaximenes* . . .'
SW 29

Antisthenes

Antisthenes (*c*.445–*c*.360 BC), a pupil of *Socrates*, was convinced that only someone who can avoid external temptations is capable of leading a virtuous life. In other words, the best happiness a human being can hope for is a form of home-made contentment, which develops and can be learnt from self-sufficiency.

Those who followed this doctrine were known as Cynics, a word which comes from the Greek *kynos*, dog. This was the nickname of the philosopher *Diogenes*, whom Antisthenes encouraged to lead a highly individual sort of life, and who became the source of many anecdotes.

'This statement {by *Socrates*} could be the motto for the *Cynic* school of philosophy, founded by *Antisthenes* in Athens around 400 BC'
SW 109

St Thomas Aquinas

He was probably not only the greatest and most important, but also the fattest, philosopher of the High Middle Ages. This, at least, is what some of his contemporaries maliciously said of him.

St Thomas Aquinas (1225–74) was born into an aristocratic family from southern Italy. He entered the Dominican Order, which had only just been founded, promulgating the ideal of all-embracing asceticism. His family had certainly planned an ecclesiastical career for him, but did not wish him to join forces with the Dominicans, an order of beggars. His brothers were dispatched to bring him back. When Aquinas refused to comply, they were not above using underhand means. The story goes that they sent a 'woman of easy virtue' to his room. However, she herself soon took to her heels, when the future father of the Church halted her advances by holding out a burning log, thus demonstrating a manliness she had not expected.

Later, Aquinas taught in Naples, Paris, Cologne, Bologna and Rome, and his fame grew apace. The Church invested great hope in this thinker, to whom faith was more serious than any other question. This was something his teacher, *Albertus Magnus*, noticed very early on. Himself a famous philosopher, the latter said of his pupil that, as the 'greatest' thinker of his age, he could 'unite' the two great names of philosophy thus far: namely, *Plato* and *Aristotle*.

The philosophy of St Thomas Aquinas is characterized by an ambitious attempt to reconcile the truth of Christian *faith* with the thought of Aristotle. As a result, faith is certainly given primary importance – something the Church very much wanted – but *reason* is also accorded more rights. It is allowed to perceive all the truths that do not emerge from revelation – in other words, below the threshold of belief, which, on earth, amounts to quite a large area.

Aquinas gave science more room for manoeuvre, which it did not hesitate to use. This, in turn, was to lead to conflicts with Aquinas. God is 'the one who exists', being in itself, uniting essence and existence. God, Aquinas believed, is the most perfect of creatures. To doubt him is not merely foolish but, in effect, impossible, for a perfect creature embodies all possible qualities, including existence – a proof of God's existence that was subsequently used by later thinkers.

God has created the world out of the void, and his Creation is well ordered. It extends from the very bottom, from matter up through the elements, plants, animals, human beings and angels – all the way to God. As the very first and very highest creature, God *is* being, while everything created merely *has* being – in other words, only borrows it for a short span of life.

Within human beings, Aquinas sees form and matter united. He regards the soul as the formal principle of physical matter, whose differences make up the various special external qualities that an individual has. In addition, however, the immortal soul also influences human beings' capacity to assimilate knowledge. With the help of a central 'communal sense' the soul is able to direct and unify incoming sensory material, as well as the thoughts that accompany it.

St Thomas Aquinas left a considerable body of writing behind him. As his sighing pupils were forced to conclude, it 'surpasses our strength' to study it all. In 1323 he was canonized. In 1557 he was declared a father of the Church, and his doctrines – 'Thomism' – were elevated to the status of an official ecclesiastical philosophy. He himself considered his work, which others held to be superlative, merely inconspicuous. Thus, as he felt death approaching, he apparently completed his working life with the words: 'I cannot do any more; in the face of what I have seen, everything I have written seems to me like so much chaff.'

'The greatest and most significant philosopher of this period was *St Thomas Aquinas*'
SW 150

Archimedes

Archimedes (*c.*287–212 BC) is considered the most important mathematician of the ancient world. This is a view he himself probably shared, as he is reputed to have had no feelings of inferiority whatever. His statement: 'Give me a fixed point to stand on and I shall move the earth!' not only confirms his phenomenal self-confidence, but also prefigures what was to become the proverbial 'Archimedean point'. From this, as if by a 'brainwave', one can proceed to a problem's solution.

Archimedes, who was employed at the court of the tyrant Hieron II of Syracuse, also made a name for himself as a highly gifted inventor. It is to him we owe such useful articles as the block and tackle, the hydrant and the burning-glass.

'Archimedes was a Greek scientist . . .'
SW 257

Aristippus

. . . .

A mysterious philosopher about whose life we have no reliable information . . . yet one of the views attributed to him always finds adherents. This is the belief that only the present – especially the individual moment – counts, something we value so long as it brings us feelings of pleasure.

'But Socrates also had a pupil named *Aristippus* . . .'
SW 111

Aristotle

Aristotle (384–322 BC) was born the son of a doctor in Stageira, on the peninsula of Chalcidice. His father, Nicomachus, was for a time First Physician at the court of the Macedonian king, Amyntas II. At the age of seventeen, Aristotle moved to Athens and became a student at *Plato*'s Academy. His relationship with his teacher, while not entirely uncomplicated, was reputedly positive. This is confirmed by the fact that Aristotle stayed in Athens for twenty years.

His hopes of becoming head of the Academy after *Plato*'s death were not fulfilled – the colourless Speusippus was appointed instead. Aristotle left Athens and moved to Assus, in Asia Minor, where he was able to continue his philosophical studies among like-minded colleagues. Here, he also married Pythias, a niece of the tyrant Hermeias of Atarneus.

After an interval tutoring *Alexander the Great* as a young man, Aristotle returned to Athens and established his own Academy, the so-called Lyceum. Here, it is said, he taught with never-failing friendliness and wrote a large number of philosophical works. When *Alexander* died, the political wind changed. Anti-Macedonian forces gained the upper hand and Aristotle was accused of 'sacrilege'. He fled, after declaring – in an allusion to the death of *Socrates* – that he did not wish to 'give' the Athenians 'the opportunity' to 'sin against philosophy a second time'. Accordingly, he spent the last years of his life in Chalcis, on the island of Eubea.

Aristotle has gone down in the history of European thought not only as the most influential Greek philosopher after *Plato*, but also as one of its first systematicians. His prodigious industry has rightly been singled out for praise. Even though only some 80 works of the 400-plus attributed to him have survived, these represent a considerable body of work. Aristotle's interests ranged over a great many different subjects. Even so, he always applied his philosophically inquiring mind to specific issues. All in all, then, we are presented with a spectrum of knowledge that retains unity within variety and focuses on the particular within the universal.

It is Aristotle's deductive reasoning, a mode of thinking which he retained all his life, that we have to thank for the real insights with which his name remains associated. Thus, he is considered the founder of formal logic, whose effectiveness lies in the fact that it does not focus on real objects, but aims instead at unambiguous conclusions arising from specific statements and concepts. Along with the 'principle of contradiction', the centre-piece of formal logic is the 'syllogism'. According to this, two interrelated statements result in a third statement that follows inevitably from the first two. A well-known example is: 'All human beings are fallible' + 'All philosophers are human beings' = 'All philosophers are fallible'.

Adronicus, who administered Aristotle's estate, classified his so-called Primary Philosophy, which featured prominently in Aristotle's overall work, and which focused on primary princi-ples and causes, as 'metaphysics' – philosophy that comes 'after physics'. Metaphysics later became a branch of philosophy in its own right, and nowadays it denotes the philosophical doctrine of what really exists and its origins.

Unlike his former teacher, *Plato*, who believed in a higher world of 'ideas', of which all earthly things are simply reflections, Aristotle believed in an immanent form that resides within an individual object and does not exist separately from it. Form is dependent on a substance that can determine it – and form and substance are interdependent. Similar considerations apply to 'possibility' and 'reality', which develop a casual connection only when certain causes – to do with effect, purpose, form or substantiality – are also present.

Aristotle tried to imagine only one exception – though a very important one – to this fundamental interdependence. This concerns the most original of all first causes, the 'primary being', the 'unmoved prime mover', who can also be called 'God'. This is a pure, immaterial form that, freed of all responsibility, enjoys and contents itself with silent contempla-tion – observing things that actually exist. Even though divine original power no longer plays any part in their everyday activities, the cosmos and life in general remain dependent on this primal force, since in the final analysis all regular patterns merely emulate the original act of creation. That said, human beings are able to get close to their prime mover – even to emulate him in a way, albeit at one remove. In other words, they, too, can devote themselves to the tranquil contemplation of things that actually exist – to *theoria*. For Aristotle, this is the most exalted of all activities, and thus also represents the highest form of practice.

Aristotle is a philosopher who detests extremes. For him, the same is true of politics and ethics. Among the forms of statehood he evaluates – all of which revolve around the idea of the Greek city-state – a moderate form of democracy strikes him as the most workable. In his view, moderation includes the presence of slaves, whose existence Aristotle regards as a natural fact of life about which there can be no argument. Except insofar as they have not been created by unjustified wars of conquest, slaves are first and foremost slaves because they have not been capable of anything else. While holding this opinion, the philosopher generously pleads that every slave should retain one grain of hope – the hope of gaining freedom.

Aristotle sees human beings as *rational* creatures, whom he recommends should behave in a rational way. This requires certain virtues that not only should prove their worth as such, but must also be valid in certain social contexts. Human action is directed towards the goal of achieving happiness. To Aristotle, in accordance with his thinking as a whole, this is also bound up with his restrained appeal for moderation in all things. For him, therefore, happiness does not mean an excess of feeling, but the certainty that one is living in harmony with reason. In the final analysis, this boils down to living a 'good life'.

'Aristotle's writings were as dry and precise as an encyclopaedia. On the other hand ... He was the great organizer who founded and classified the various sciences ...'
SW 89

St Augustine

St Augustine (354–430), whose real name was Aurelius Augustinus, was born in Thagaste, North Africa (now Souk Ahras, Algeria). His Christian mother, Monica, influenced him more than his pagan father, but initially without any measurable success. When young, St Augustine read Latin poets, especially Cicero, but had difficulties with Greek, which remained a closed book to him throughout his life. He transformed Cicero's recommendation to study philosophy into a personal quest for truth, something which, initially at least, he was free to do.

Accordingly, he joined the controversial *Manichaean* movement, whose radically dualistic attitude to life promised him a fundamental choice of good or evil. He studied rhetoric in Carthage, was given a teaching post there, and then, against his mother's wishes, went to Rome. His professional success culminated in the rank of imperial 'rhetor', a kind of orator, at the court in Milan.

Thereafter, he began to distance himself from worldly affairs. He separated from his partner, with whom he had been living for more than twelve years, and by whom he had a son. He was converted to Christianity in 386. This conversion is one of the best-known key experiences in the history of philosophy, about which St Augustine later wrote in his most famous book, the *Confessions*.

At Easter 387, he and his son were baptized by St Ambrose, Bishop of Milan. St Augustine returned to Africa and, with like-minded colleagues, established a community in his native town of Thagaste. This community was devoted to communal living and studying. In time, he was also appointed Bishop of Hippo Regius (now Annaba, Algeria). He died at the age of 76 while Hippo was being besieged by the Vandals.

St Augustine wrote more than 90 books, as well as innumerable letters and sermons, which left his first biographer to conclude that no mortal could ever read all his works.

Philosophers regarded St Augustine's acute analyses of time as essential reading. Although he himself had for many years believed in a higher authority, St Augustine urges his own epoch to focus on what it can be most aware of – an individual's sensibility. The 'ego', he believed, stands in the river of time, where it must learn to understand that its past 'no longer' exists and that its future has 'not yet' begun. That said, the apparently most real segment of time – the present – loses itself in a welter of extremely brief moments that are whisked away again almost before they have been experienced. The special way our consciousness is constructed – a structure that reveals God – is our only foothold in the swift-flowing river of time. More specifically, human beings have been given memory, which means that they retain images of their past. Further, by making projections from the present, they can prefigure the future. The interplay of time-strata in human consciousness creates experience. This, in turn, opens up a mental perspective to us, whose enigmatic complexity could also be equated with God.

The philosophy developed by St Augustine, who may also be considered as the thinker who coined the term 'original sin', had an enormous influence on the Church's official religious canon. In the final analysis, his strict doctrine of grace, which hardly leaves the individual any room to achieve eternal life by taking actions pleasing to God, made people more fearful than joyful. If, as St Augustine asserts, everything is merely the work of God, then even those good deeds that one has done with pride and a good conscience lose much of their inner justification and are, in the final analysis, worthless.

'. . . and we might as well begin with *St Augustine*, who lived from 354 to 430 . . .'
SW 146

Francis Bacon

Bacon (1561–1626) held high civil service offices that left him time to write philosophical works. All of these express a new-found conviction that human beings have only just begun their journey along the path of knowledge and are capable of achieving more – a great deal more.

The climax of Bacon's political career came when King James I arranged for him to be appointed Lord Chancellor. This position became null and void only three years later, in 1621, when he was found guilty of taking bribes and had to resign from all his offices.

As a philosopher, Bacon was concerned with looking at reality in an unprejudiced, clear-sighted way – a view which helps establish a form of knowledge that takes humanity further. Unlike God, who – thankfully? – does not have these problems, human beings are always liable to be victims of error and misjudgement. Bacon's exposition of the 'Idols of the Mind', set out in his book, the *Novum Organum*, can be read as a way of avoiding prejudices and false philosophical systems.

' "Knowledge is power," said the English philosopher *Francis Bacon* . . .'
SW 169

Baroque
· ·

As a period in intellectual history, the Baroque mainly encompasses the seventeenth century, in which the experiences of the Thirty Years War shaped people's feelings about life. Death and destruction vied with visions of raw vitality. As for God, people believed he was back in his accustomed position among – or, rather, above – humanity. Two Latin mottoes encapsulate the twin poles of an attitude to life typical of the Baroque period, which achieved a makeshift tranquillity. They are: *memento mori* ('remember we must all die') and *carpe diem* ('grasp the day, enjoy the moment').

'The Baroque . . . "We are such stuff as dreams are made on . . ."'
SW 190–1

Simone de Beauvoir

The partner of the philosopher *Jean-Paul Sartre*, Simone de Beauvoir was often – usually by male colleagues – regarded as his appendage, which resulted in her being given a malicious nickname, 'Notre Dame de Sartre'. Later, people were forced to revise their overhasty opinion, at least to some extent.

Simone de Beauvoir (1908–86) showed herself to be a personality in her own right. When occasion demanded, she was able to bring some of her friend's more high-flown philosophical projects a little nearer earth – through a combination of precise criticism and repeated reminders that a realistic view of the world also had its advantages. In her own philosophy, de Beauvoir kept faith with women's issues. These she did not wish to hand over wholesale to combative committees intent on 'raising consciousness' and run by overzealous feminists. As she herself said: 'No one should believe that the female body gives you a new vision of the world. That's absurd. Women who believe that are merely falling back on irrational, mystic, entertaining realms. They are playing men's games . . .'

'He met his life-long companion *Simone de Beauvoir* in a café . . .'
SW 378

George Berkeley

When only fifteen years old, George Berkeley (1685–1753) became a student at Trinity College, Dublin, a well-respected academic institution. Here, his fellow students got to know him as a gifted young man with a tendency to precociousness. He studied ancient languages, as well as philosophy, mathematics and – last but not least – theology. In 1707 he was ordained a priest. His first piece of philosophical writing, which appeared in 1709 and promised 'a new theory of perception', did not appeal to the reading public – not least because readers objected to his ponderous style and his preference for obscure turns of phrase.

Berkeley vowed to improve his style, revised his first work and only one year later published a greatly improved and extended version, which went down better without becoming a runaway success. Only with a newly revised version of *A Treatise concerning the Principles of Human Knowledge*, which this time he couched in the form of a dialogue, did Berkeley achieve the recognition for which he yearned.

Now, he was glad to discover, he could travel with a clear conscience. This he did extensively, until he was appointed Dean of Derry and, following his marriage, needed to settle more permanently. Berkeley allowed himself one last major trip in 1729, when he voyaged to the Bermudas. Here, he wanted to fulfil a long-cherished wish to found a missionary school that would train the sons of English settlers along with young men born in the locality. The project failed, and Berkeley returned to Ireland a disappointed man. He saw his appointment as bishop of Cloyne in 1734 as an act of compensation, and he remained in this post until his death.

Berkeley was one of the earliest philosophers to accord the human mind much more than the mere assimilation of impressions perceived by the senses. According to Berkeley, *consciousness* is the only substantial stage on which the action of the world can take place. What happens away from this stage is of no great interest because it does not take place in the conscious mind.

Berkeley does not question the fact that the world is composed of matter, but he does dispute its independence from the human mind. For him, all the qualities that ordinary things possess are different ingredients of consciousness, and they become essential to the lifelong process of acquiring experience.

This radical form of *idealism*, which retains its room for manoeuvre by making concessions to the material world, had a stimulating effect on philosophical debates at that time, when theories of perception were just beginning to emerge. In the process, readers often chose – sometimes accidentally – to overlook the theological guarantee underlying Berkeley's philosophy. His thesis was that the finite mind of human beings originated in the infinite mind of God, and was kept in working order by God's creator-mind. Our conscious mind only works because it is meant to work. In the final analysis, therefore, we can regard it as a gift that God made long ago to all human beings in what is for them their only world.

'Berkeley . . . like a giddy planet round a burning sun . . .'
SW 234

Big Bang

. . . .

In 1929 the American astrophysicist Edwin Hubble noticed that distant galaxies were moving away from our Milky Way – at a speed that is all the greater the further the galaxies are from the constellations in our solar system. Hubble concluded that the cosmos is still expanding. The implication of this is that earlier – very much earlier – galaxies must have been much closer together.

From these observations, scientists developed the theory of the 'Big Bang', according to which the cosmos was created some 20 billion years ago in a sudden explosion. This Big Bang may well have been the start of everything – space, time and matter.

This theory is not accepted by everyone – just as there are many other partly proven or totally unproven speculations in the realm of cosmology. After all, human beings were not present at the creation of the cosmos. Nor will we still be there when, at some distant date, the universe shuts up shop.

Human beings simply have to live with this uncertainty, along with several others. In the meantime, if it helps, they can console themselves with the insights that philosophy provides. With regard to our knowledge of stellar worlds, we must heed the words of Harald Fritzsch, a German professor of physics. Fritzsch says: 'We have to accept that there are no absolutely enduring structures in the cosmos. Everything is in constant flux, and all structures eventually dissolve.'

The ancient philosopher *Heraclitus* would have very much enjoyed hearing this.

'We call this explosion the Big Bang . . .'
SW 421

Jakob **Böhme**

··

Trained as a shoemaker, Böhme was a German mystic, who expressed his profound thoughts either by saying nothing or in obscure, picturesque language.

Böhme (1575–1624) believed in the absolute unity of the divine, which can be sensed only if contrasts exist that can be related to one another. This means that the conditions essential for life can exist only in terms of contrasts. Light reveals itself only against darkness, good needs evil in order to be truly good.

In the final analysis, even God is dependent on this infinite chain of contrasts. He cannot raise himself and emerge from the heavy burden of his obscure origins until he is given the opportunity to reveal himself in a totally different form.

'. . . the Romantics were tracing their roots not only back to Spinoza, but also to . . . Renaissance philosophers like Jakob Böhme . . .'
SW 290

Niels Bohr

. . . .

Bohr (1885–1962), who won the Nobel Prize for Physics in 1922, showed more interest than most of his colleagues in problems connected with the theory of knowledge. He tried to give his own special 'reading of how atoms worked' a universal application. This he attempted to achieve by questioning the structural basis – and, in the final analysis – the credibility of a form of knowledge which, in the case of an atomic model, for instance, proved something was potentially 'there' without actually showing it.

The concept of 'complementarity' which Bohr developed suggests an innate interrelation of viewpoints that may at first sight seem opposite or contradictory.

'. . . the Danish nuclear physicist Niels Bohr is said to have told a story about Newton's having a horseshoe over his front door . . .'
SW 306

Giordano Bruno

....

A contemporary documentary source described Giordano Bruno (born 1548), who was burned in Rome on 17 February 1600, as a 'criminal Dominican' and an 'exceedingly obstinate heretic'. Enemies of Bruno, a former monk who was always fearless and dogmatic, considered him merely quarrelsome, whereas his admirers regarded him as a saintly philosophical figure.

Bruno believed in the overriding power of reason as the supreme creative principle of the cosmos. For him, this all-powerful reason embraces the concept of the world-soul, which extends into the most minute parts of the living world. This attitude to life leaves no room for God, whom Bruno imagined to be a supra-sensible being beyond human understanding – a view that led inevitably to conflict with the established Church. The last words that Bruno spoke – clearly for posterity – at the end of his trial have become famous: 'You pronounce your verdict with greater fear than I accept it.'

'The fate of Giordano Bruno was a dramatic example of this {the idea of pantheism} . . .'
SW 168

Siddharta Gautama **B**uddha

Buddha (*c*.560–*c*.480 BC), the founder of Buddhism, was the son of a prince who came from what is now Nepal. At the age of 29, so the legend goes, he abandoned wealth, a beautiful young wife and a delightful little son and set out to search for salvation. He wandered about as a beggar, called on a number of hermits who were considered wise, and submitted to all manner of ascetic regimes. That said, he found truth only when he discovered his own enlightenment – a doctrine he then conveyed to others in the style of a humble wandering preacher who could work miracles.

Buddha ('the enlightened one') lived the doctrine he preached, and he did so in such a way that at first no one asked any questions about a personal God or gods. Buddhism (SW 127) is a religion that manages without a supreme master of the universe and has little patience with time-honoured notions like the self – the ego – or even the soul.

Buddhists see existence much more as a process of continual evolution – the 'wheel of becoming'. There are no fixed substances, but merely a pattern of birth and extinction. This pattern is marked by suffering and always goes beyond the key experiences of existence, such as birth and death. Buddhists believe in reincarnation and the cyclical pattern of life. The only way to break out of this cycle is to annihilate the self in 'Nirvana', a state of supreme calm and stillness when all desires have ceased.

'Buddha saw life as an unbroken succession of mental and physical processes which keep people in a continual state of change . . .'
SW 227

Queen Christina of Sweden
....

The daughter of Gustavus Adolfus, the legendary King of Sweden, liked to match herself against men – not least in the fields of philosophy and the fine arts. Christina (1632–54) assured her place in philosophical history – even if it was a little outside the mainstream – when she gave René Descartes, the famous philosopher, a position at her royal court as an adviser and intellectual guiding force.

At court, she made the philosopher, who was by then 54 years old, rise early. Accustomed to staying in bed till noon and to day-dreaming, Descartes found that the harsh Nordic climate not only put him in a permanently bad mood, but gave him a chill, which turned into pneumonia and finally killed him.

Christina, who tended to make sarcastic remarks, is said to have greeted the news of his death with the words: 'My illustrious tutor promised me that with the help of science he would live to be a hundred. He has failed to keep his word.'

'In 1649 he was invited to Sweden by Queen Christina . . .'
SW 195

Marius Tullius Cicero

The philosopher and statesman Cicero (106–43 BC) lived an eventful life, in which politics led to excitement and philosophy to reflection. He held the office of Consul and made sure that the Catiline Insurrection was put down. In the civil war, however – as history was to show him in due course – he temporarily backed the losing side. It took an act of mercy on the part of Caesar, the victor, for him to escape with his life.

As a philosopher, Cicero felt closest to the Greeks. Without many misgivings, he followed those teachings that seemed best suited to his own philosophical world. This he conceived on a grand scale – and the things that interested him most were death, life, friendship, love and eternity. Cicero practised philosophy as a continuing means of acquiring wordly wisdom. His – now lost – manuscript *Hortensius* is said to have influenced *St Augustine* and started him on the path towards philosophical meditation.

'As a Roman philosopher, Cicero, said of him a few hundred years later, Socrates "called philosophy down from the sky and established her in the towns . . ."'
SW 58

Marie Jean Antoine Nicolas Condorcet

Condorcet (1743–94), the mathematician and philosopher, believed that anything feasible could be considered reasonable provided it 'sufficed' to reconcile 'a liberal constitution' with 'the universal education of all citizens'. This, however, was easier said than done. In pre-revolutionary France, the obstinacy of the privileged classes was almost beyond belief. That said, when the French Revolution finally succeeded, fanatics so distorted his plan that the Marquis de Condorcet's educational ideal turned into something far less sublime.

This intrepid *Enlightenment* philosopher's origins in mathematics, which remained his favourite science, were apparent in all his political projects. He always underpinned his political visions with statistics and probability calculus. Even so, the aims connected with them – equality for women, science serving humanity in rational and beneficial ways, the liberation of all those who were oppressed, and justice for all – were almost entirely beyond reproach.

'As early as 1787 the Enlightenment philosopher *Condorcet* published a treatise on the rights of women . . .'
SW 263

Consciousness

The question of consciousness is not necessarily the oldest problem facing philosophy, but it is one on which opinions are often divided. To address the problem we need to ask very basic questions of ourselves. How do we see the world, and how do we see ourselves – if knowledge of ourselves and of the world comes to us only through the consciousness we are given along with our bodies? Unlike our awareness of our own bodies, consciousness contains within it opportunities for development that can lead to what we now call 'self-discovery'.

Consciousness is always awareness of some object. This is equally true of self-consciousness, which, presumably, is a mysterious variant of consciousness. At the same time we must acknowledge that the self – a fluctuating though constant entity that controls our thoughts and behaviour, without our having to gaze into a crystal ball – is not just an object like everything else.

In the history of philosophy, *Hegel*, that most German of all German philosophers, made the heaviest demands of consciousness. For him it was the absolute spirit, which, in the final analysis, knows everything and sees through everything – especially Hegelian philosophy. Nowadays, people prefer not to make demands of that kind. Despite this, and however difficult it proves to be, philosophy ought to explore the discoveries of modern research into consciousness. These are promising and at the same time disappointing.

Julian Jaynes, the American psychologist, has formulated a thesis that is relevant here. According to him, consciousness may be simply a phenomenon of the mind that appears occasionally by accident, having first emerged about 3,000 years ago. It might, in his view, just as accidentally disappear again one day in the distant future . . .

'That's why we often say or do things without intending to. Unconscious reactions thus prompt our feelings and actions . . .'
SW 362

Nicolaus Copernicus

The man who brought about the so-called Copernican Revolution led a quiet life, notable for its friendly relations with other people. From the outset, the wealth of his parents meant that he had no material problems, so that he could devote himself to his studies, which ranged widely.

Copernicus (1473–1543) studied mathematics, physics, astronomy, medicine and ancient languages. In due course, he was even granted a doctorate in canon law. At first, his insights struck him as so far-fetched that he hesitated before publishing them. He did not want to make himself 'look ridiculous', but, cautious by nature, he was probably also reluctant to take issue with the Church.

That said, he formulated his crucial finding early in his career: 'All planetary bodies orbit around the sun, as if it stood in the very centre of the cosmos, and thus the central point of the universe lies near the sun.'

He finished his uneventful life in surroundings from which legends can grow. He lived in a tower at the Castle of Frauenburg in the Ermland, East Prussia. Here he used to write and reflect, and only allowed one woman to visit him. This was his housekeeper, Anna Schilling. At the time, it was rumoured that they were linked by something more than domestic duties.

'Copernicus claimed that it was not the sun that moved round the earth, it was vice versa. '
SW 170

Charles Darwin

A single voyage – though one that went on for five years – was what inspired the otherwise sedentary Charles Darwin (1809–82) to develop a new picture of the world whose consequences we still cannot foresee.

Darwin, the son of an important country-doctor, was an inconspicuous schoolboy, who did not attract attention to himself either by special brilliance or by any pranks he played. He used to collect beetles and was a keen bird-watcher, but he was also just as happy losing himself in his day-dreams, in which he 'often forgot who [he] was'.

He was equally unobtrusive as a student. He studied theology, medicine, zoology and geology in Edinburgh and Cambridge, without feeling the degree of enthusiasm which, on a good day, he demonstrated while engaged in hunting. Eventually, in 1831, he was persuaded to take part in the voyage that was to change his life. His Majesty's Research Vessel, HMS *Beagle*, which was bound for South America and the East Indies, was looking for a young scientist to be ship's naturalist. Darwin accepted the offer.

Darwin coped with the conditions on board ship, the lack of space, the constant swaying of the ship ('which at first made me permanently sea-sick') and, above all, the mood-swings of the choleric Captain Fitzroy, better than had been feared. In the course of his work, which he found more and more interesting as time went on, he developed colossal enthusiasm and a remarkably conscientious approach.

By the time the *Beagle* returned to England in October 1836, Darwin claimed to know exactly what 'the value of life' was. He catalogued the biological specimens he had collected during the voyage. He also got married, fathered ten children and worked as a secretary, private tutor and writer. His first bestseller was the published edition of the account of his travels.

Darwin never suffered money-worries – his father's legacy often made him financially independent. Nevertheless, his main work, *On the Origin of Species by means of Natural Selection*, did not appear until 23 years after the end of the great voyage. That is how long Darwin, a highly scrupulous researcher, needed to expand his theory into a book, which now created an enormous sensation. On the very first day of publication, the first edition sold out, and the work became the most-read scientific work of the nineteenth century. He was only marginally involved in the heated debates that his theory unleashed. He wrote various other books, read bulky novels ('which must always have a happy ending'), and finished living his uneventful life. On the day before his death he is rumoured to have said: 'I do not have the slightest fear of dying'.

Darwin is considered the founder of the biological theory of evolution. According to this theory, living creatures are subject to a process of natural selection, in which the best-adapted organisms – those able to adjust to the conditions prevailing in their environment – are most likely to survive. Darwin found all kinds of proof for his theory while voyaging on the *Beagle*. The Galapagos islands in particular, which he called 'a world in themselves', offered him a wealth of visual material.

Darwin's thesis was as follows. The 'struggle for survival', which all forms of life have to undergo, is an instinct innate within any species. Through a process of procreation and mutation, only the fittest examples of a given species can survive. These are then exposed to a fight for survival on a higher plane – a struggle with other animals and plant-species.

Reduced to simple terms, therefore, the history of evolution could be read as a family chronicle that mainly features victorious types. 'Social Darwinism' has acquired some of these characteristics, and has adapted certain aspects of the theory into the alleged superiority of races allegedly better equipped for survival.

Darwin himself, who lost his usual equanimity only when he spoke of the subject he detested above all others – namely, slavery – would have had great difficulty with these attempts at interpretation. For him, the theory of evolution meant little more than statistics of survival. That said, these data needed extremely careful evaluation, as does his theory of the origin of species.

'The situation was comparable to what happened later on when Darwin proved that mankind had developed from animals . . .'
SW 176

Democritus

Democritus (*c.*460–*c.*370 BC) called himself 'worldly-wise'. He travelled extensively and, so he maintained, he learnt a great deal. He is said to have had a cheerful disposition – in marked contrast to the permanently sombre mood of his colleague, *Heraclitus*. Democritus has earned his place in the history of philosophy as the second Atomist – the first being his teacher, Leucippus.

Atoms form the building blocks of the cosmos. As such, they are different from one another in weight, size and form, but indivisible. They move through empty space, and as they collide, but before they coalesce into specific groupings of atoms, they form the world of real objects.

Human beings also consist of atoms, and if they wish to feel at peace with themselves their 'soul-atoms' must be kept stable and free from shock. People can themselves ensure that this happens, for they are responsible for their own souls. In this regard, they even have a certain freedom that is almost entirely lacking in the otherwise overregulated natural world.

'Today you are going to hear about the last of the great natural philosophers. His name is *Democritus* . . .'
SW 37

René Descartes

Before becoming a philosopher, Descartes (1596–1650) was a professional officer. He served in the army of Prince Moritz von Oranien, and there, if we believe his biographers, he made a name for himself as an audacious swordsman. At the same time, even in those early days, people praised this short man's brilliance. He was able to solve complex mathematical problems in a matter of minutes, he always spoke about theoretical physics as if his words were about to be published, and he also wrote personal notes, whose content he hardly ever divulged.

Descartes was educated at the highly respected Jesuit college at La Flèche. At the request of his father, a ponderous lawyer and civil servant, he studied jurisprudence in Paris, which did not stop him from pursuing his pleasures. In 1618 the Chevalier du Perron, the name Descartes now took after unexpectedly inheriting an aristocratic title, began training to be an officer in Holland. At that time, this country was especially advanced in military technique and was also considered the most liberal land in Europe. On a November night in 1619, when the Prince of Orange's army was encamped in winter quarters near Neuburg on the Danube, Descartes had his key philosophical experience. This consisted of three successive dreams that showed him, in a pictorial message, the direction his future life was to take.

He quit the military, went back to France to become a man of science, and soon had a reputation for performing miracles. Even though neither the ecclesiastical nor the state censor's offices had any specific grounds to arrest him for subversive writings, in 1628 Descartes thought it advisable to return to Holland once again. He stayed there for over sixteen years, which, all things considered, were his happiest – not least, perhaps, because he experienced love there, whereas previously he had known only casual affairs. In the last years of his life Descartes became famous throughout Europe. He died at the court of *Queen Christina of Sweden*, who resolutely admired the philosopher, even though she greatly overestimated his powers.

Descartes taught philosophers to (re)turn their attention to themselves. He did this by being audacious enough to make his own self the starting-point for all subsequent considerations, which initially had only one object in view: the reliability and certainty of knowledge. The technique he adopted was his method of universal doubt, which he applied to everything that could possibly be disbelieved. As a child of his time, a period of healthy scepticism towards confirmed truths, Descartes was well aware that the process of doubting should not be taken too far.

Thus, when he had completed his critical examination, two truths, which were more or less sacrosanct, remained. These were – hardly surprisingly – God; and the self, the 'I'. This, Descartes believed, could not automatically be taken as a centre of certainty. Descartes' famous formula, 'Cogito ergo sum' ('I think, therefore I am') uses an artifice in order to confirm the self as a thinking being, the *res cogitans*, before which, so the argument runs, doubt must, in the final analysis, capitulate – since nothing can be doubted if the doubter himself does not exist.

From this fixed point of certainty we can derive all other definitions of reality. The self as a thinking being is faced with the world of *substance*, the *res extensa*. This comprises all aspects of objective reality – not only *nature* and society but also the body, which Descartes explicitly describes as an object distinct from the process of thinking. Body and soul may well be yoked together in mortal existence. Yet they are totally different from one another, and in their respective functions. We can see this clearly when a human being dies. The soul leaves the body and sets out to join God, while the mortal remains show how perishable they are by decaying where they lie.

Descartes even allocated a specific organ in human beings to the everyday interaction between body and mind. This is the pineal gland, the epiphysis cerebri, which is aware of its controlling function from its position at the rear of the forebrain, the diencephalon.

The dualistic attitude to life that Descartes' philosophy developed had – and still has – something seductive about it. Modern sciences, of which philosophy probably counts as a foster-parent, immediately succumb to its charms. For if the self and its *vis-à vis*, substantial matter, are clearly separated from each other, patterns of realistic perception become possible. The self, that thinking, exploring, insatiably inquisitive being, can build up a fund of knowledge. Because this knowledge is derived from concrete objective sources, it can lead on to aspects of truth that can be evaluated and on which we can count.

Without exactly wanting to, Descartes' philosophy has lifted the veil of secrecy from the world. Ever since, the world has become an object of scrutiny – not only for those seeking knowledge. The mysteries that still exist show a different kind of obscurity. Yet curiously enough they – still – relate to those two truths that Descartes though he had excluded from the process of doubt, namely God and human *consciousness* – two areas of truth that philosophy still fails to address adequately.

'Descartes . . . he wanted to clear all the rubble off the site . . .'
SW 194

Dialectics

··

The traditional form of dialectics is the classical triad, which consists of thesis, antithesis and synthesis. It serves to advance an argument by helping it through self-evident contradictions in existing assertions. As a method, therefore, dialectics is dependent on the willingness of its user to make certain propositions – and this makes it seem somewhat arbitrary. In their time, dialectical arguments have made some audacious assumptions. This is especially true of the philosophy of what used to be called Communism, which – without taking any losses into account – sought to explain, in dialectical terms, not only history and world-conditions, but also human beings' behaviour far into the future.

Hegel, one of the old masters of dialectics, had already criticized the effectiveness of this kind of prognosis, and he called the dialectical method an 'externally lifeless mechanism'. By expressing his reservations in this way, Hegel was indirectly alluding to early dialectics in the works of *Socrates* and *Plato.* Both these philosophers used dialectics to release a process of thought by means of dialogue. This process would lead to a gain in knowledge as certain positions were first adopted, then, as the process went further, challenged.

'. . . But Hegel's dialectic is not only applicable to history . . .'
SW 304

Diogenes

Diogenes of Sinope (*c.*400–325 BC) is one of the first philoso-phers to become an object of ridicule. He marks the start of a kind of anti-history of philosophy, in which philosophers are seen as unworldly and eccentric, and – so runs the unspoken assumption – nothing very illuminating is to be expected of them.

That said, Diogenes presumably had a good mind. Whether he really used to live in a barrel, while surviving on next to nothing and being extremely rude to people, we cannot say with any certainty. What we do know is that he was given the nickname of 'kynos', 'dog' and a whole school of philosophers – including Diogenes' teacher, *Antisthenes* – was named after him.

One of the best anecdotes about Diogenes brings him into contact with *Alexander the Great*. In a condescending but friendly manner, the King asked him what he most wanted, to which Diogenes brusquely replied: 'You to stop blocking my light!'

'The best known of the Cynics was *Diogenes* . . .'
SW 109

Ecophilosophy

Ecophilosophy is closely bound up with the ecological move-
ment, which it supports philosophically in its fundamental
concern about environmental problems. That said, ecophiloso-
phy is more interested in clarifying moral or ethical issues than
concepts that have a bearing on the future.

The history of philosophy has always paid some attention
to the relationship between *nature* and spirit, and between
human beings and their environment. However, it was un-
able to face the ecological crisis with which we are now
confronted.

That said, there were several warnings – not least from
Heidegger, that controversial philosopher. In his late philo-
sophy, he reminds us not only of the 'forgetfulness of being',
but also of our increasing intellectual impoverishment. In
Heidegger's view, human beings have settled into intellectual
laziness, concentrating so much on their own immediate
successes – which for Heidegger are based on 'calculating
thoughts' – that they forget their real natures. Thus, they
haven't even realized that the spectres they used to conjure
up now refuse to go away. 'The meaning of the technological
world', Heidegger writes, 'remains hidden . . . But a far greater
danger now threatens us – at the precise moment we have
averted a Third World War. This may appear a strange asser-
tion at first – but, if we think hard about it, it will begin to make
sense . . .'

Heidegger continues: 'My assertion holds insofar as . . . the
Technological Revolution might so captivate, bewitch and blind
people that one day human beings will be capable only of
calculating thought . . . Then, the most sophisticated and
sharply focused form of calculated planning and invention
would coincide with utter indifference towards deep thought –
utter thoughtlessness, in fact. Which would mean? That human
beings had denied and thrown away their essential characteristic
– their thinking nature. This is why we must save this precious

part of the human psyche. This is why we must keep thought alive.'

'A central philosophical direction in the twentieth century is therefore *ecophilosophy . . .*'
SW 384

Empedocles

Empedocles (*c*.495–*c*.435 BC) was multi-talented. He was active as a statesman, doctor and faith-healer. According to *Aristotle*, he was also the real inventor of rhetoric. Although an aristocrat, he was in favour of democracy, to which his home town of Acragas (Agrigentum), Sicily, objected so fiercely that he was declared *persona non grata*.

Philosophically, Empedocles did the four elements – fire, earth, air and water – enormous honour. According to him, they are everlasting and present in all other things. Together with the creative principles of love and conflict, which are not subject to any time-constraints either, the four elements determine how the world will develop. As it does so, it moves and 'mixes' – a process that sets Empedocles apart from his colleague, Parmenides, and his Eleatic School.

In the fragments attributed to Empedocles we find a great many astonishing, in some cases staggeringly modern, suggestions. Thus, for instance, he writes about a kind of collective Fall, caused by universal human sinfulness and punished by degeneration into 'physicality', as well as by the endless wandering of the soul, which Empedocles saw as a restless, 'fallen god'.

'It fell to Empedocles . . . to lead the way out of the tangle they had gotten themselves into . . .'
SW 31

Empiricism

∙∙

Unlike *rationalism*, which saw itself embellished by *reason*, empiricism laid great stress on the original power of the five senses. According to empiricists, any communicable view of reality must originate from our senses. They provide us with the sense-data that lie at the root of our acts of perception.

If one wishes to express it that way, empiricism was founded by *Epicurus*, and was then extended to embrace experience of the world in general by the British philosophers *John Locke, David Hume* and *John Stuart Mill*. Their countryman *George Berkeley* – slightly against his better judgement, perhaps – also contributed.

Empirical knowledge, as comprehensive and well protected as possible, has become the ideal of the exact sciences, which, obeying their own necessities, long ago developed far beyond classical empiricism.

'. . . What a lot of difficult words! Could you repeat the meaning of empiricism? . . .'
SW 217

Enlightenment

The Age of Enlightenment, which spread a special atmosphere of a new beginning, focused on *reason*, encompassed the seventeenth and eighteenth centuries. A definition that has since become classic of what the Enlightenment might mean was provided by the philosopher, *Immanuel Kant*: 'The Enlightenment marks a human being's break with self-inflicted immaturity. Immaturity is the inability to use one's mind without another person's guidance.'

Even so, Kant continued, only after immaturity had been transformed into maturity could the mind realize how hard it is to manage without 'another person's guidance'. A person's capacity for knowledge, now freed of all self-appointed authorities, is thrown back on its own resources, and this is both a challenge and a responsibility.

'The Enlightenment . . . from the way needles are made to the way cannons are founded . . .'
SW 261

Epicurus

Ancient chroniclers of philosophical history sometimes liked to embellish the truth. In the case of Epicurus (341–271 BC), they maintain that he became a philosopher while still a precocious boy. At school he is said to have asked where 'chaos came from'. An exasperated teacher supposedly replied: 'We can't know that. It's a question philosophers are wrestling with!'

At this, Epicurus apparently left school immediately to become a philosopher and, we might add, to found his own school. For quite a long time the philosophy he presented attracted a great many followers – probably in part thanks to the teacher. Epicurus was often praised for his friendliness – especially towards ordinary people. Several philosopher-colleagues, whom he tended to treat in a less friendly way than people in the street, reproached him for this unintentionally democratic manner.

Central to Epicurus's philosophy is pleasure, which he regards in a more complex way than *Aristippus*, who thought that pleasure could be attained only in moments of fulfilment. Epicurus distilled the concept of pleasure into an attitude to life that is governed by prudent moderation. It avoids extremes, refuses to chase after sensual pleasure and, instead, advocates a well-thought-out form of self-restraint. His motto was 'Live unobtrusively!' In essence, therefore, pleasure means something more akin to contentment, whose motivation can simply be the absence of pain and displeasure.

All things considered, Epicurus believed, human beings are not offered much else by way of happiness. They should be glad to get through life in a more or less healthy state – spared the really major, gruelling emotions. Once people have grasped this they can attain inner peace, which Epicurus denotes by the lovely Greek word *ataraxia*, meaning 'equanimity' or 'freedom from anxiety'.

Epicurus's philosophy is both empirical and practical in its application. The same goes for his theory of knowledge, which trusts the evidence of sensory perceptions. As a rule, our senses give us reliable information, out of which we can construct an orderly picture of the world. Only atoms escape the net of our perceptive powers. First, they are too small and secondly – unlike the atoms about which *Democritus* writes – they move freely and at exceptional speed.

If historical sources are to be believed, we owe Epicurus several enduringly wise sayings. One of these maintains that it is senseless to be afraid of death, for 'when we exist there is no death, and when death exists there is no us'.

'... Around the year 300 BC Epicurus ... founded a school of philosophy in Athens ...'
SW 111

Erasmus of Rotterdam

Unlike *Martin Luther*, who manoeuvred himself out of the Catholic Church in order to carry through his reforms, Erasmus of Rotterdam (*c.*1466–1536) remained within his religious community. Because Erasmus was not only a humanist but also a very keen philosopher and, in religious matters, a great philologist, he was able to see things in broader perspective than Luther.

Human beings are certainly dependent on the grace of God, but they also have some freedom of movement – especially when it comes to doing good. Only in such cases, when their actions remain free, do the good things they do – especially the good things performed unselfishly – reveal themselves to be worthwhile from the perspective of morality and the commandments, which apply to each individual while also being valid on a universal basis.

'There were also ecclesiastical reformers who chose to remain within the Roman Catholic church. One of them was *Erasmus of Rotterdam* . . .'
SW 177

Eros

Eros, the son of Aphrodite, was originally an early Greek god of love, whom the Romans called Cupid. In some writers' stories he appears to be stealthy, even insidious. He is young and good-looking and creeps about with a bow and arrow or sometimes with a burning torch. No one can feel safe from him, which probably accounts for a lot of the attraction of love.

Later, Eros was depersonalized and thus stripped of his unpredictability. *Plato* turns him into an ethical and aesthetic motive force: insofar as he symbolizes the struggle for what is good and beautiful, Eros increases human happiness. First of all, however, so the philosopher tells us, people must raise the level of this happiness – from the depths of physical desire to the higher sphere of the mind, from where one can enjoy sublime views of the universe of ideas.

'Plato calls this yearning *eros* – which means love . . .'
SW 75

Ethics

In its early forms – the philosophy of *Aristotle*, for example – ethics is synonymous with practical philosophy. Among other things, this asks what a 'good life' consists of, and what a human being must do to live within the bounds of reason – which obviously always means more than the well-being of a single individual.

Understood in this way, ethics amounts to far more than an individual's claims to happiness and moral conventions. It also has to encompass society and the state, as well as the moral values which – for whatever reasons – are acknowledged by a given community.

In time, ethics as a philosophical discipline became more specialized. It focused more specifically on personal criteria of behaviour, examining the extent to which its subjective motives might be reconciled with objective circumstances.

In our own day, ethics faces difficult questions posed by the perspective of what is possible. Despite being responsible for an unexpectedly vast advance in knowledge, human beings feel insignificant and helpless. This is because they are now faced with decisions about whether they may do all the things they are capable of. Future ethical discussions might well recall the emphasis on human sympathy that Arthur Schopenhauer (1788–1860) – among other philosophers – thought important. From the suffering in which creatures languish everywhere, Schopenhauer created a sobering imperative to love one's neighbour.

'The ethics of both Plato and Aristotle contain echoes of Greek medicine . . .'
SW 97

Existentialism

....

The term itself suggests what we are discussing: human existence, that timeless and mysterious reality which is often where philosophy begins. Among other questions, existentialism asks: do human beings – now and unfortunately for ever – have only themselves for company?

If true, this statement confirms humanity's ever-recurring alienation. Even though it starts from an obvious point of departure, the individual self's mode of existence, existentialism has never made much impact in the world at large. A certain unease seems to develop when people focus too closely on the narrow circle of their own activities.

The true founding father of existentialism was probably *Kierkegaard*, but the analyses of different aspects of time which the Church father, *St Augustine*, completed also form part of a good existentialist's standby rations. In the twentieth century, the philosopher and writer *Jean-Paul Sartre*, has been most instrumental in helping existentialism flourish once again. That said, however, his brand of existentialism proved to be more a matter of modishness than an optimistic fresh start for philosophy.

'Existentialism, inspired by the Danish philosopher {*Kierkegaard*} , flourished widely in the twentieth century . . .'
SW 319

Faith

. . . .

Faith has a truth all of its own, independent of the normal means of proving something to be true. In this sense, the old adage 'Faith can move mountains' has some truth in it. As this saying suggests, faith is closely related to belief – certainty born of profound inner conviction or advice that issues from a higher, divine source.

In its usual form, then, faith bears a strong resemblance to religious conviction. Quite apart from this, we can call upon faith for almost any quality or phenomenon. This can lead to a mysterious 'strength of mind', which well-known sportsmen-philosophers, such as Boris Becker, can summon.

It should come as no surprise that faith no longer plays much part in the history of philosophy. Philosophy itself can be seen as a valiant attempt at intellectual emancipation, which might lead from belief to knowledge. In a sense, though, we encounter a certain coyness here, for the more we think we know, the less knowledge reveals of its real mysteries.

'Fundamental questions such as these can only be approached through *faith* . . .'
SW 316

Johann Gottlieb Fichte

Fichte (1762–1814) became a philosopher by accident. It was thanks only to a private stipend that this son of a poor artisan was able to attend school and later study theology. Throughout his life he was never free of money-worries. Like many of his colleagues in those days, he had to offer his services as a private tutor in order to make a meagre living. When one of his students asked for lessons in *Kant*'s philosophy, Fichte, who knew very little about philosophy, was obliged to take a crash course in the subject. He studied Kant's writings day and night, always interpreting them in a highly individual way.

In time, this accidental introduction to philosophy was crowned by success. In the meantime Fichte had made contact with the good-natured philosopher in person, and he asked Kant to help him find a publisher for his first work: *Attempt at a Critique of All Revelation*. This début volume, which was indeed published with Kant's help, appeared anonymously. Ironically, it was taken as the long-awaited new work by Kant, the illustrious Königsberg philosopher, and was greeted with appropriate interest. When Kant, who was not only good-humoured but also magnanimous, revealed the mystery surrounding Fichte's book, it was Fichte's turn to be famous.

Although Fichte came late to philosophy he rapidly achieved success in spite of himself, in his profession. He became a professor – first in Jena, then in Berlin. Always convinced about the importance of his own person, he expressed this in a series of public statements. Much to his disappointment, however, his 'Addresses to the German People', which he delivered to his audience in all good faith, aroused very little interest. Fichte's philosophy presents a consistent line of *consciousness*-theory, and as such it is an integral part of German *idealism*. It promotes the self – the 'I' – to the status of a creative force, which not merely is responsible for everyday thought-processes in the human mind, but also constructs a world that transmutes ideas into objective reality.

As something that originates in the mind, the self is initially absolute – the 'absolute I'. However, this self may not be content to remain absolute, but be obliged to force itself into the world and take on a real, individual form. In this form the self 'posits' a non-self, a 'not-I'. Absolute consciousness expands and creates several objects for itself – including nature, for instance, but also the 'empirical self', which is divided among a very large number of different minds. The resulting process, whereby reality is consciously constructed, takes us back to the very beginning. In other words, the absolute self, released into the world of objects, nature and finite consciousness, becomes genuinely – 'intellectually' – conscious of itself. It is no longer purely absolute, but only relatively absolute – in empirical terms, it is determined by reality.

Fichte himself often varied the philosophical basis of what he called his 'Science of Knowledge' because – so he believed – it ought to provide the 'basis of all knowledge'. In every new draft, Fichte made his 'Science of Knowledge' more abstract, extending it a bit further towards heaven – and this process also enhanced its resonance of meaning.

In the 'Age of Rational Science' that he had inaugurated, Fichte wanted to prove his credentials as a 'practical' philosopher by – among other things – realizing what he called the 'closed trading state'. This, we assume, would be scrupulously fair – offering equal education to everyone – but also rather dour. All things considered, the resulting community might have resembled a locked hall with guards on the door and a notice saying: 'Private, Keep Out'.

'The philosopher *Fichte* said that nature stems from a higher, unconscious imagination . . .'
SW 293

Marsilio Ficino

··

This son of a doctor initially became a doctor himself, and as such earned his living for a while. At the same time, however, he was a committed philosopher. In the 'divine *Plato*' and his followers – mainly *Plotinus* – he sought to find the reassuring and unifying power that could forge a bond not only between human beings and God, but also between different religions and cultures.

Ficino (1433–99) taught at the Academy in Bologna, and in 1473 – because of a different form of commitment – he was ordained a priest. He was responsible for the first complete translation of Plato into Latin, and made a name for himself as a sensitive commentator on his master's works.

As in Plato's concept of *eros*, Ficino accorded love a special role. It should not, Ficino insisted, waste itself in everyday sensual activity, but join the soul on its upward flight into higher reaches – to a sphere in which the soul is no longer troubled by physicality. Here, sublime contemplation of the divine ensures – or so he claimed – everlasting well-being.

'One of the central figures of the Renaissance was *Marsilio Ficino* . . .'
SW 166

Freedom

So long as they have time and leisure, and have no major anxieties about how to live, human beings generally regard themselves as free. This also means that many people believe in free will – though this is a belief not everyone holds. Understood this way, freedom means human beings' fundamental opportunity to make decisions for themselves. In more recent times, this freedom to make one's own decisions, which applies equally to body and mind, has become an indispensable idea, which is understandably considered an inalienable right.

Freedom becomes problematic only when it shifts away from the individual who lays claim to it and is meant to apply to whole societies – even states and national communities. In these cases, freedom becomes a disputed force for good, a watchword open to different interpretations, which means one thing in the jargon of people in power and quite another in the language used by those who are oppressed.

In the history of philosophy, German *idealism* has probably developed the most far-reaching concept of freedom. Its sophistication lies in the fact that it combines an external lack of freedom with a hugely inflated freedom of thought, whose potential for subtle interpretation can hardly be increased. In recent times, the notion of freedom has been treated more pragmatically.

Nowadays, we need to remember that freedom is not just a word, not merely an overworked, often abused value. It can also raise awkward questions when applied as an abstract assumption to people – in the so-called Third and Fourth Worlds, for instance – for whom simple survival means so much more than a mere word.

'. . . But only when we know in ourselves that we are acting out of respect for moral law are we acting freely . . .'
SW 278

Sigmund Freud

The founder of psychoanalysis was a doctor, a psychologist, a philosopher and – above all – a practitioner, who collected and codified his discoveries into a method. This became a means to treat patients and – as was to be maliciously proved later – even people who were well.

Freud (1856–1939) spent nearly 79 years in Vienna, his chosen home, which he left only when forced by the Nazis to emigrate to London. The success enjoyed by psychoanalysis – it has declined somewhat in recent years – rests mainly on the fact that human *consciousness*, which often seems chaotic, can be 'explained' in terms of the unconscious, which can be made responsible for any sort of problem. The unconscious is like a vast storage shaft of the soul where everything is filed away and stockpiled – discarded knowledge, obscure instincts, anxieties, desires, fragments of dreams. It also stores all the behaviour-patterns that result in various forms of coercion, as well as the frequent small slips people are always making during their lives.

The discovery of the unconscious, for which Freud cannot take all the credit himself – other philosophers, including Schopenhauer, were there before him – made it possible to look at the human psyche as a whole. Most importantly of all, it now became possible to explore the psyche in an objective, methodical manner.

If we look at the psyche in two parts, we can first see it in terms of the 'unconscious, pre conscious and conscious', all of which form the background to the ego's identity. Secondly, we can see how Freud envisages the 'id', which embodies human drives and sensual needs, and the powerful 'super-ego', by which Freud understands the pressures to fulfil expectations and to conform that all individuals have to acknowledge.

Between these areas of the psyche a kind of competition rages as to which area will be more repressive. The struggle is governed by a kind of regulatory activity that the individual seldom – if ever – understands. This is why, as soon as any disturbance comes to light, he or she needs the help of a therapist, who can provide analysis to turn vague assumptions into certain knowledge.

Some psychoanalysts are skilled in the art of identifying manifestations of the soul, which they have suggested to their patients in the course of analysis. However, deep psychological examination has shown its success in another, very obvious way. The terms used by Freud have rapidly become household words, and even nowadays these words are invoked whenever psychic issues are explained in a halfway competent manner.

The same applies to other discoveries that Freud made, such as *Jokes and their Relationship to the Unconscious*, to which even mediocre jokers refer. This insight of Freud's is as illuminating as the proverbial 'Freudian slip' or the 'reality principle', which is used to browbeat all those people who refuse to give up futile day-dreaming, desires, absurd ideals and even obsessional habits.

Finally, Freud's analysis of dreams, which attempts to unlock repressed material by interpreting specific symbols, has unearthed a lot of evidence that has influenced other fields of scientific study.

'. . . Freud's studies of the unconscious revealed that people's actions were often the result of "animal" urges or instincts . . .'
SW 337

Galileo Galilei

· ·

Galilei (1564–1642), a physicist, mathematician and astronomer, turned *empiricism* into a scientific discipline. Previously, especially in its biological forms, it had been characterized by unshakeable dogma – with the Church its principal advocate.

A professor in Pisa, Padua and Florence – which still did not solve his chronic financial problems – Galilei took the bold step of speaking up for the new heliocentric solar system formulated by *Copernicus*. This theory contradicted the traditional view of the universe, with the earth at the centre of a fixed cosmos controlled by God.

As the guardian of the true faith, the Holy Office instituted legal proceedings against Galilei. He was compelled to recant in public and was placed under house-arrest. This might seem a relatively light punishment, but in fact it was a major defeat with far-reaching consequences.

Although, after his trial, he had to come to terms with tormenting self-doubt – as well as questions about his steadfastness under cross-examination – Galilei proved strong enough to stand by the method he had devised. This insists on the need for empirical findings, which, together with an all-encompassing theory and – repeatable – philosophical experiments, can be extrapolated in such a way that scientific advances can result.

Galilei sought to describe the world exactly as it is. Accordingly, when describing scientific data, he is obliged to concentrate on 'primary' – that is, measurable – qualities, and to ignore all the 'secondary' extras, as perceived on a personal basis.

As an astronomer, Galilei discovered Jupiter's satellites, which were subsequently named after him. As a physicist, he founded cinematography with his theory of motion.

'. . . the Italian Galileo Galilei, who was one of the most important scientists of the seventeenth century . . . was roughly contemporary with Kepler'
SW 169, 171

Georg Wilhelm Friedrich Hegel

Hegel (1770–1831) was a late developer. As the eldest of three children in a German civil servant family, he had senior status for a long time. While studying theology at the Tübinger Stift, where he became friends with *Schelling* and Hölderlin, he was given the nickname, 'the old man'. And in later years, when he was a professor of philosophy, most of his colleagues were much younger than he was. Hegel compensated for this 'disadvantage' by his tenacious perseverance – his strength was that people tended to underestimate him.

After completing his studies, he worked as a private tutor in Berne and Frankfurt am Main. Then, recommended by Schelling, who was five years his junior, he progressed to a professorship in Jena. Later still, the political situation obliged him to work in a different place and at a different profession. First, he became editor-in-chief of the *Bamberger Zeitung* (newspaper), then Rector at the Aegydiengymnasium (grammar school) in Nuremberg.

Thereafter, Hegel started on his highly individual path towards renown. In 1816 he was appointed professor of philosophy in Heidelberg, where he taught for two years. He spent the rest of his life in Berlin. By now he was the best-known philosopher in Germany. His lectures were to some extent cult-events, even though he was no great orator. As a commentator once said: 'H. did not speak smoothly, or fluently; he would croak, clear his throat or cough at virtually every phrase, and was always correcting himself . . .'

Hegel died from the after-effects of a cholera epidemic that raged through Berlin. When he died he may not have been the oldest, but was probably one of the most famous, victims of the epidemic in Prussia. Hegel gave philosophy the organized shape that *Kant* had advocated earlier, making the whole structure more systematic and rounding it out. Probably only a very German philosopher – an audacious civil servant of a philosopher – could have undertaken such a monumental task.

That said, the starting-point of Hegel's thought, namely that we must think the 'thoughts of God before Creation', reveals an intellectual exorbitance cloaked in profundity. In his system, Hegel wanted these thoughts to lead us to supreme reason, completing a process of self-knowledge sparked off by the 'spirit' or 'mind'. Spirit or mind is most evident in *consciousness*. It creates the infinite variety of the world of ideas in the intellect; though Hegel in no way denies the other side of life – reality, the objective world.

Nevertheless, reality always needs its own form of knowledge in order to 'realize' itself. Only when it is perceived, or 'known', can reality be considered 'rational'. An expert *dialectician*, Hegel juggles contradictory statements, all of which he integrates into a thought-process that shapes and determines everything. Subjective and objective spirit or mind, individual and supra-individual consciousness overlap with one another, so that human beings are in the final analysis just cogs in the whirring gears of world-history, whose monumental machinery goes on running from the start of time to the very end of Creation.

Individuals are hardly more than vehicles of consciousness, whose value is measured against others of their kind – an infinite number of other insignificant vehicles of consciousness. A human being's personal well-being, happiness or distress are of no interest whatever. Accordingly, Hegel can write: 'World history is not a breeding-ground of happiness. Moments of happiness are blank pages in it . . .'

In all his ebullient honesty, with its dash of outrageousness, Hegel is one of the strangest and at the same time most fascinating figures in the history of philosophy. No other philosopher has ventured to corset the world so tightly in rigorous thought, and yet in no other philosophy are sublime and massive concepts so near to being reassuringly intimate.

Like Faust, Hegel has at least two different souls residing in his breast. Further, if we remember that Hegel drank prodigious quantities of wine, we might dare to speculate that Hegel, the philosopher, may have had a Doppelgänger. In this scenario, the adventurous explorer of the intellect would be complemented by a respectable citizen who put his feet up in the secure knowledge that he was famous. Thus, we would have a Dr Hegel and Mr

Hegel, a thinker who internalized his dialectics, yet at the same time gave it a tangibly everyday form.

Nor should we forget that, although Hegel's writings are not exactly gripping to read, on a good day he could also coin a memorable phrase. Thus, he once observed: 'Trying to perceive something before we know how to perceive anything is as foolish as learning to swim before we have dipped our toe in the water.' We might also care to recall an occasional passage such as 'The dissolving away of the exquisite but unreal soul . . . in consumptive yearning'.

'Hegel . . . the reasonable is that which is viable . . .'
SW 299

Martin Heidegger

Heidegger (1889–1976) is still one of the most controversial thinkers of the present day. This is largely because he was involved with Nazism, after which – much to the disgust of his admirers – he expressed hardly a word of regret for his political misjudgement.

This did not detract from Heidegger's renown. Alongside *Kant* and *Nietzsche*, he ranks as the best known of all German philosophers throughout the world. Oddly enough, his fame is greater outside his homeland than within it. In his early works Heidegger was concerned with analyzing the situation in which human beings find themselves as they choose between death and dread of life, between anxiety and boredom. His late philosophy, however, directs our attention to human 'forgetfulness of being', and this takes Heidegger into memorably fundamental territory.

In exploring the question of how and where truth 'manifests itself', Heidegger reaches beyond the sphere of the subject and, with a dramatic gesture, goes back to primal sources.

Although Heidegger spent most of his life working in the provinces – chiefly the Black Forest region – and outwardly cultivated a certain peasant guile, he also presented himself as an admonishing figure, who criticized the way people exploited *nature*. In his own words: 'The world now seems like an object attacked by calculating ideas. Nature has degenerated into a colossal petrol station – a source of energy for modern technology and industry. Long ago, these powerful forces grew well beyond the scope of people's will and ability to make decisions.'

'A man who was influenced by both Kierkegaard and Nietzsche was the German existential philosopher *Martin Heidegger*'
SW 378

Hellenism

The period normally called Hellenism can be specified fairly exactly. It extends from the death of *Alexander the Great* in 323 BC to the second half of the first century BC, when Greece was breaking up and being absorbed into the Roman Empire.

External decline was balanced out by the spread of Greek culture. This proves the point that words and actions can have an effect even when they are not words of command or military actions.

'Hellenism . . . a spark from the fire . . .'
SW 102

Heraclitus

··

Heraclitus (*c.*540–*c.*480 BC) is one of those Greek philosophers about whom more anecdotes are in circulation than reliable information. One explanation for this is his character, which seems so hermetic that chroniclers had to exercise their own imaginations. We must also remember that only some 80 fragments by Heraclitus have survived, and these show that their author – although wise – was rather obscure, making him difficult to follow.

Heraclitus was reputedly born into a royal family in Ephesus, whose privileges he apparently spurned. Instead, he went in search of the truth. This, however, turned out to be a fruitless task for him and – if contemporary witnesses are to be believed – he is the philosopher who inaugurated the whole idea of ill humour. He thought humanity capable of very little except its usual wickedness. But despite rejecting his privileged background, he could never entirely abandon his aristocratic roots. His philosophy always has a high-handed, overbearing tone, and, when in doubt, he would rather risk a confident assertion than attempt moderately to see both sides.

Unlike his colleague, *Parmenides*, who denies that things move, Heraclitus maintained that 'everything was in constant flux'. Further, he believed that the element of fire was the primal constituent of the cosmos. This is everlasting, he asserted, and creates units of mass – from the large masses of land, sea and sky to the small, finely structured fabric of the soul.

Heraclitus also liked to explore contradictions, which, he thought, can help foster reality. This method influenced other philosophers, including *Hegel* and *Nietzsche*. The overbearing side of his philosophy emerges chiefly from his advocacy of war, which he addresses as the 'father of all things' and 'the universal'. Finally, however, Heraclitus reaches the laconic conclusion: 'War reveals that some people are gods, others, human beings; some it makes slaves, others free people.'

Despite all the stupidity in human life, there is, Heraclitus maintains, a kind of 'law governing the world', which he calls the *logos*. Originally this meant 'meaningful speech' or *reason*, but for Heraclitus it represents a solitary, primitive power to create, which will be 'obscure to many', but which, we assume, he could comprehend.

Heraclitus's cryptic ambiguity has inspired several writers. Many of his statements invite us to murmur and brood. They include: 'Human beings often light a lamp for themselves at night when they have already died but are still alive' and 'The way up and the way down are one and the same.'

'A contemporary of Parmenides was *Heraclitus* . . .'
SW 30

Johann Gottfried Herder

Herder (1744–1803) was not, according to the writer Jean Paul, 'a star of the first magnitude', but a 'whole galaxy, out of which . . . everyone selects one particular constellation at will'. And it is certainly true that Herder's philosophy – he was principally a theologian who worked for a long time as a general superintendent in Weimar – had a rather laboured and arbitrary quality about it, which his contemporaries, including Goethe, never quite accepted.

Nor was Herder very systematic. He tended to follow the inspiration of the moment, and so it comes as no surprise that his philosophy of history, for which he became well known, emphasized the rights of various cultures and nations, all of whom were equally far from – or near to – 'God'.

Herder countered the prevailing *Enlightenment* view, which was well meaning but fallacious, that everything could now be known about everything. Instead, he insisted that there had to be by-ways through history. He also believed that there were residual areas of mystery that no human being could elucidate.

Herder became very well known as a philologist. He believed language capable of much more than most of his contemporaries did. As he himself said: 'Only when we speak does reason assert itself.'

'A man who came to have great significance for the Romantics was the historical philosopher Johann Gottfried von *Herder* . . .'
SW 292

Herodotus

....

Cicero described him as the 'father of history'. Unlike his colleague *Thucydides*, Herodotus (*c.*484–*c.*424 BC) was a historian who only rarely allowed himself elaborate digressions. Instead, he often urged his readers to act morally. This, he believed, would be possible only if people behaved with moderation – similar moderation was necessary to avoid shipwreck on the seas of history.

In his *Histories*, Herodotus tells us what happens when people act immoderately. He also shows us that powerful individuals who try to emulate the gods end up being powerless. It is incumbent on people, Herodotus thought, to chronicle key instances of human success and failure, 'so that posterity will not forget what happened to people in the past'.

'The best known Greek historians were *Herodotus* . . . and *Thucydides* . . .'
SW 46

Hildegard of Bingen

Abbess of her own nunnery on the Rupertsberg near Bingen, Hildegard (1098–1179) was one of the very few leading women of her epoch. She always behaved modestly, exaggerating her ignorance and god-given inferiority as a woman. However, this did not stop her expressing her opinion and at times putting her foot down.

Hildegard was a gifted natural scientist, and was also active as a doctor of medicine and preacher of sermons. Her philosophy is characterized by *inspiration*, and she considers it most important that she 'receives' her 'visions; not in 'dream-states or sleep', but 'awake, level-headed, with a clear mind'.

Hildegard's philosophy is well disposed towards human beings who, because this is God's will, can reflect the world and the ocean of the sky.

'But that did not mean that there were no women thinkers. One of them was *Hildegard of Bingen* . . .'
SW 155

Hinduism

. . . .

Hinduism, a religion practised mainly in India, Pakistan and Bangladesh, manages perfectly well without any specific founder. It sees itself as 'eternal' and can accommodate a plethora of gods, demons and saints.

Hinduism teaches that the rich diversity of the world – and of living creatures – is organized in a hierarchic structure, over which a higher justice, the law of 'karma', rules. According to everyone's secret merits, each individual reaches the place he or she 'deserves', so that complaints are pointless and cannot be accepted.

Hinduism relates to *Buddhism* in its doctrine of the transmigration of the soul, but uses this as a means of justifying the caste system.

'. . . we can see a number of clear parallels between Hinduism and Buddhism on the one hand and Greek philosophy on the other . . .'
SW 127

Hippocrates

A mysterious figure, Hippocrates (*c.*460–*c.*370 BC) was a Greek physician who allegedly provided a whole profession with a statement of ethical intent, the 'Hippocratic Oath'. Very little is known about his life – even anecdotally.

That said, some treatises attributed to Hippocrates have survived. These indicate a mind cultivated on a broad scale, which ranges from surgery to pharmacology and anatomy, and encompasses medical welfare in general. As a physician, Hippocrates trusted his intuition, which enabled him to recognize symptoms of illness and draw universal conclusions from them.

As a philosopher, he is said to have formulated many fine aphorisms, such as this one, which neatly summarizes the complexity of life: 'Life is short, art long; the right moment quickly passes; experiences are deceptive, decisions difficult.'

'The founder of Greek medicine is said to have been *Hippocrates* . . .'
SW 47

Thomas Hobbes

Hobbes (1588–1679), who came from a humble background, was not popular as a philosopher. This was because he thought human beings capable of every kind of atrocity. 'Homo homini lupus' ('Human beings are wolves to other human beings') became his best-known statement.

Hobbes was looking for more than merely a social theory – he was attempting a systematic summation of all objective reality, which he intended to inventory by mathematical methods. In completing these calculations, Hobbes reduced human beings to numerical figures. However, in the light of his other views – see above – this hardly seemed to matter.

Yet despite the low opinion he had of human beings, Hobbes saw them as individuals, as 'subjects' in their own right, whose independence is vital to a well-regulated, lawful, trading state. The state is given the thankless task of balancing out its members' malice and wilfulness in such a way that the 'commonwealth' can be established, a task which only a very powerful state – the 'Leviathan' – can achieve. As Hobbes himself writes: 'From this institution of a commonwealth are derived all the rights and faculties of him, or them, on whom sovereign power is conferred by the consent of the people assembled.'

'Materialism also had many advocates in the seventeenth century. Perhaps the most influential was the English philosopher *Thomas Hobbes* . . .'
SW 192

David Hume

. . . .

Hume (1711–76) came from a strict Presbyterian background, in which so much extreme piety reigned that no one ever asked for explanations, let alone reasons.

On enrolling at the University of Edinburgh, Hume got to know as much as was then feasible of the world of books and ideas, which plunged him into profound uncertainty. His parents and relatives urged him to study law, which he conscientiously began to do. Then, however, in a fit of audacity, he abandoned these studies – and opted for philosophy. He paid for this courageous step by catching a bewildering, presumably psychosomatic illness, which caused him to suffer skin-rash, hyper-salivation and extreme loss of appetite. The latter soon reverted to its opposite, however. He was overwhelmed by an uncontrollable greediness, so that the puny, lanky youth grew into a plump young man.

Hume travelled a good deal – to France, for instance, where he worked as a private tutor and freelance philosopher, among other things. By the time he came back to Britain, he had the manuscript of his first book with him. This became an impressive failure. The exploration of human nature that Hume presented in his *Treatise of Human Nature*, its published form, 'fell dead-born from the press'. A review of the time urged readers to 'return this uncouth Scot to the obscurity' he deserved.

Only in his later works did Hume achieve a breakthrough, although at first he was honoured more as a national economist and historian than as a philosopher. He was also active in political circles, working as an Embassy Secretary in Paris and as an Undersecretary of State in the Foreign Office in London. Then he became bored and packed himself off to his father's estate in Berwickshire. In Edinburgh, towards the end of his life, he was accused of sacrilege. Because of his 'irreproachable conduct and certain strengths of character', however, the charge was dropped.

Hume is considered the foremost mind within British

empiricism. He is unwaveringly confident that the human mind can provide so many 'impressions' and 'ideas' that, together, they can constitute a form of knowledge. 'Sensible' perception, he believed, creates the basis of everything that is perceived. The more 'complex' ideas of which human beings are capable are also dependent on perception. Such ideas are meaningful only if they are based on original material that can be proved empirically. Otherwise they deteriorate into mere fantasies and are of no interest.

The self also needs a constant supply of data from the external world, without which it remains an empty shell, an abstract aspect of *consciousness* whose main value lies in its lifelong 'custom or habit'. The self always needs to know something both about itself and about the world. In its successive experience of different states of consciousness, it is a restless spirit – or, as Hume puts it, 'nothing but a bundle or collection of different perceptions, which succeed each other with an inconceivable rapidity, and are in a perpetual flux and movement'.

Just as the self depends on the process of 'custom or habit', the same applies to the relationship of cause to effect. A 'demonstrative' cause, which has taken a specific form 1,000 times, might take an entirely different form the 1,001st time. This means that all the data people assume are unchangingly regular also remain merely 'probable' assumptions, which need constant confirmation.

As a moralist, Hume trusted 'sentiments' more than mere 'reason'. In a heart-warming thought, he expresses how closely attached he feels to other human beings: 'This sentiment can be no other than a feeling for the happiness of mankind, and a resentment of their misery . . .' From this feeling emerge emotions of 'sympathy', which demand that we offer help to others even if qualities that are 'useful or agreeable to the person himself' advise against such action. As we have already said, Hume was a friendly, good-natured person. However, he always seemed to know where the real enemy of serious philosophy lurked: 'Be a philosopher; but, amidst all your philosophy, be still a man', for, as Hume maintained elsewhere: 'A wise man . . . proportions his belief to the evidence.'

'As an empiricist, Hume took it upon himself to clean up all the woolly concepts and thought constructions . . .'
SW 223

Idealism

··

In the history of philosophy, idealism is regarded as the most stylish variant of thought. It is not content merely with what already exists, but embodies a higher form of truth which – no matter how – is concerned with *consciousness*.

Thus, we cannot say that idealism makes things easy for itself. Quite the reverse, in fact. *Materialism* and *empiricism* both have an easier time of it, since they start from things that actually exist, and are in that sense realistic. There is something inherently élitist about idealist philosophies, which can seem condescending at times because they consider themselves sublime and superior to the limited grasp of an 'ordinary' intelligence.

That said, throughout the history of philosophy idealism has been responsible for all of the major ideas and most of the far-reaching and audacious projects. Idealists have probably been in a better position than other theorists to respond to that yearning of the soul which human beings drag about as they grope around in a – generally – rather miserable existence. Surely, this yearning asks, there must be something that outlasts us, a certainty that promises us some consolation before we die – a light at the end of the tunnel?

'As I have already mentioned, some philosophers believed that what exists is at bottom spiritual in nature. This standpoint is called idealism . . .'
SW 191–2

Inspiration
· ·

If, as might well be the case, our *consciousness* is only the tip of
the iceberg, below which a great deal more exists – such as the
*Freud*ian unconscious, for instance – then we should not be
surprised if we experience impulses that seem to emerge from
nowhere.

Such instants of inspiration are a law unto themselves. They
brook no contradiction and they are unlikely to reveal anything
else about the reason or cause behind their unexpected appear-
ance. Key philosophical experiences – such as those of *St
Augustine, Descartes* and *Rousseau* – owe a lot to inspiration.
The philosopher *Nietzsche* has probably described their impact
most strikingly: 'You neither listen nor look; you don't ask who
is making you the gift; an idea suddenly strikes you like a flash of
lightning in the form it inevitably has to take – I myself have no
choice in the matter . . .'

'This is when we have 'lifted the lid' of the unconscious. We can call it *inspiration*,
Sophie . . .'
SW 367

Irony

You might well describe *Socrates* as the old master of irony, insofar as he practised it in its original sense – *eironeia* is the Greek for reproach – as a refined form of dissimulation. Others have concentrated more fully on the subtle distinction between surface and substance, pretension and reality.

To express these differences verbally, one could critize something head-on. Yet it is better to use irony. This allows one to emphasize aspects that almost escape notice – by ironically inflating the opposite case, which then assumes an importance it does not actually have.

Irony has a special place in *Romanticism*. It was built up into a philosophy of life that plays with essential truths – seriously and mockingly at once. Friedrich Schlegel saw irony as a downright frivolous form of knowledge, 'which surveys everything from a great height, looking down on all created things – even on one's own art, virtue or genius'.

The philosopher *Sören Kierkegaard* demonstrated that in the right context irony can be considered witty. His ideas have certainly found very few imitators – with the result that philosophy remains rather short on wit.

'Socrates could feign ignorance – or pretend to be dumber than he was. We call this Socratic irony . . .'
SW 56

Jesus Christ

He stood for what his name expresses – the Greek form of the Hebrew word *Jeshua* – in other words, Jahwe (God) will help. Jesus Christ embodied this message in both words and actions. For all that, he remained a mysterious figure. The reports we have in the New Testament are not sufficient to give us a picture of the historical Jesus that would convince the sceptics, of whom, as we know, there are a large number.

Further, the Bible's message is one-sided – in the positive sense of the word. It appeals to *faith*, to everything that is done in its name – the acts of kindness, the healings, the miracles. What is beyond belief merely reinforces a certainty established long ago, even if it could never win over the fault-finders.

Jesus presented himself as a preacher who knew how to weigh his words and who had many possibilities at his disposal. He could be harsh and strict, as well as gentle and loving. He knew when to take action and when he needed to speak. He came into conflict with those in authority when he refused to accept the traditional system with its arrogant narrow-mindedness over class and spiritual issues.

The doctrine he preached also achieved something else. Anyone proclaiming the kingdom of God on earth, a unique event anticipated with pomp and circumstance – and anyone making the hitherto austere, blustering Old Testament God into a God of love, whom people can suddenly take to their hearts – must expect the Old Believers to object.

All things considered, then, it is possible that Jesus's presumption, which he did not always cloak in humility and kindness, was his downfall. This presumptuous tone can even be detected in the expression he often used early in his sermons or addresses. 'Verily, I say unto you' does not suggest that he expected any of his utterances to be debated or criticized.

'Both Jesus and Socrates were enigmatic personalities, also to their contemporaries . . .'
SW 57

Immanuel Kant

Kant (1724–1804) was the right philosopher at the right place. He did not pursue philosophy part time, but as a full-time professor in Königsberg. And he seemed simply to have been waiting for his opportunity to come. He was ready when it did – as he himself said: 'I shall start my work now and nothing will stop me.'

He took up the best ideas contemporary thought had to offer, and adapted them into his own philosophy, which offered a new and, above all, convincing form of knowledge at a high level. Kant was a sufficiently industrious intellectual to achieve everything he set out to do. He certainly had the 'interests of humanity' at heart, but in other respects he remained modest, since he did not wish to 'find' himself 'less useful than an ordinary worker'.

Coming as he did from a poor background – he was the fourth of eleven children in an artisan family – Kant knew poverty at first hand from a very early age. Thanks to his natural gifts and the occasional subsidy from outside, by the age of sixteen he was able to enrol at Königsberg University. Here, among other subjects, he studied mathematics, sciences, theology and philosophy. He reputedly earned the university fees by giving private coaching and from his skill as a billiards player.

After his father's death, he saw no alternative to working as a private tutor. In 1755 he returned to the university, obtained his doctorate with his first dissertation, 'Concerning Fire', and completed his post-doctoral thesis shortly thereafter. Although small in stature, Kant was considered a colossal intellect. That said, he was too modest in his behaviour to draw undue attention to himself.

There followed long years of conscientious work – as a university lecturer and occasionally a librarian. Then, in 1770, his commitment to his work – always full of dedication – was rewarded with a full professorship in metaphyscis and logic at Königsberg University. This removed everyday financial anxieties, and he concentrated on his life's work, philosophy, for as long as his 'life-clock' would continue to tick.

Kant asked himself the – always pertinent – questions of philosophy, which appear straightforward but are in fact extremely intricate. This is why these questions still lead to almost obsessive philosophical speculation. They are such questions as: 'What can I know?' – 'What am I to do?' – 'What dare I hope for?' – 'What is a human being?'

Kant started by trying to put knowledge on a more or less stable footing by arbitrating, like King Solomon, on the philosophical dispute between *empiricism* and *rationalism* – deciding whether *consciousness* or reality played a more important role in acquiring knowledge. Equipped with certain forms of 'understanding' and 'observation', so Kant believed, human beings who seek knowledge approach the real world, which provides them with sensory data. These 'transcendental' forms – such as space and time, cause and effect – exist 'a priori'. In other words, they stand independent of our 'sensibility' and are thus 'universal and necessary'. Imposed on the phenomena we perceive, these forms determine our experiences.

Thus, with the help of their perceptive faculties, human beings bring a certain order to things, which can therefore appear to them only as they perceive them. In other words, human beings look at things through spectacles, as it were, which see them as they appear and which, irrespective of their transcendental structure, reveal the viewers' genetic pre-programming. Accordingly, we can perceive the real world of objects only in a limited way. We cannot perceive 'things in themselves', and we can only perceive things at all if we acquire knowledge as part of a community, with a collective experience that adjusts to our limited means of perception.

This pattern of knowledge needs to seem convincing as it has to include the assumptions that people will sooner or later think out for themselves – that there is a reality which is independent of us. To the best of our ability, however, we form a picture of it with which we can live and work, and which can even help us make progress. Everything that lies beyond human beings' horizon of perception becomes 'speculative'. This does not mean it is either useless or meaningless. God, the soul, the world are 'determinative ideas', which serve our knowledge as timeless, valuable benchmarks.

To the question 'What am I to do?' Kant also provides an illuminating answer. Human beings should base their actions on *reason,* which points them beyond selfish behaviour and sets them on a course of action that will benefit the whole community. The most important guiding principle for rational behaviour – because it satisfies moral dictates – is the 'categorical imperative', which has become especially famous. In its more extended form, this can be described as follows. 'Act in such a way that the maxims of your will can always be considered a principle of universal legislation. Act as if your will can transform the maxims that govern your personal actions into universal laws of nature. Act as if you are using humanity – both in your own person and in the person of every other individual – as an end, not merely a means.'

Specific good or bad deeds are left to the individual, whose 'duty' is to decide one way or the other. The categorical imperative provides only a rough rule of thumb, and specific do's and don'ts have to be related to it. The excuse that people have to act as they do because a human being is subject to the dictates of reality cuts no ice with Kant. As rational beings, Kant argues, human beings are free, and can rise above things. They can also overcome obligation. Their conscience tells them the same: 'You can do it because you should!'

The question as to what human beings dare hope for is something Kant passes on to religion, of which he expects a certain tolerance. 'There is only one true religion', he believes, 'but there can be many different kinds of faith.' Religion, he continues, need not 'unthinkingly wage war' against reason, for 'it cannot conquer it'. In the final analysis, therefore, the kind of religion Kant prefers is a form of rational religion tailored to the individual. This form of religion remains open to 'beauty' and to what is sublime and great. To find solace and abiding hope in this religion does not require us to think overwhelming thoughts. Quite the reverse. Something insignificant can set the process off: 'The silent stillness of a summer evening, when the quivering light of the stars breaks through the brown shadows of night and the lonely moon stands within the circle of our face.' In the same vein, Kant tells us elsewhere that 'little by little . . . sublime . . . sentiments of friendship, of contempt for the world, of eternity are gradually drawn out . . .'

As for what a human being really is, Kant lays this question at the door of 'anthropology'. He himself never liked to step outside the realm of reason, whose validity he supported even within the limitations of what is 'human, all too human'. Yet despite his good nature, Kant sometimes allowed himself slight touches of malice. On one occasion, for example, he noted: 'One might almost think the human head was really a drum which only makes a sound when it is empty.' However, he immediately added, in a more generous spirit: 'We mustn't tread on one another's toes; the world is big enough for us all.'

'After Hume, the next great philosopher was the German, Immanuel Kant'
SW 260

Johannes Kepler

· ·

Kepler (1571–1630) was, among other things, a professor in Graz, where he was responsible for a rather unusual combination of academic subjects – mathematics and moral sciences. All his life he remained pious, and accordingly, unlike his colleague, *Galilei*, he earned his living from the Church.

He first discovered the laws governing planetary motion, and these were later named after him. He also played a key role in developing the astronomical telescope.

In a work exquisitely titled *The Secrets of the Universe*, he set out his philosophy. Its point of departure is a form of cosmic harmony in which God, the clandestine architect, can make himself felt as a real presence through familiarity with the magnificent diversity of his creations.

'But in the early 1600s, the German astronomer *Johannes Kepler* presented the results of comprehensive observations . . .'
SW 171

Sören **K**ierkegaard

With the arrival of Kierkegaard (1813–55), a fresh wind blew into philosophy, which until then had been increasingly weighed down by systems of thought. A theologian by training, Kierkegaard set out to balance far-reaching explications of the world against the problems of the individual, which philosophy had tended to overlook.

Kierkegaard had his key philosophical experience – the 'great earthquake' – while still a student. What exactly this shattering experience was is something experts still dispute. Presumably it was his discovery of the guilt that was hanging over his parental home. Whether this was a sexual misdemeanour, a divine curse or simply a deceptive manoeuvre must remain an open question. At all events, it was Kierkegaard's father who was the guilty party, and the son shared his feeling of guilt.

Both father and son were of a melancholy disposition. This characteristic can often lead to exceptional clear-sightedness, and Kierkegaard described it as 'quiet desperation'. All his life he was dogged by guilt-feelings, and he saw his existence as one long error of judgement. Theology, which he conscientiously finished studying after his father's death, was no help to him, and so he felt obliged to follow the freelance career of a writer and philosopher.

Kierkegaard lived in Copenhagen and strolled about its streets – soon becoming a familiar figure whom people greeted with a smile. No one dared to approach him directly, for he was known as someone who could be sharp-witted and malicious. For two months be persevered with an engagement to be married, which he had begun when he still believed himself capable of a middle-class life. When the engagement was broken off, the only person to be surprised was Kierkegaard's fiancée. Once it was all over, Kierkegaard felt free to write whatever he liked, however desperate.

In his works, which have such expressive titles as *Either/Or*, *Fear and Trembling* and *The Concept of Dread*, he turns his own inner doubts into philosophical events. Human beings, he maintains, are constantly faced with fundamental decisions that demand a confession – to oneself, to the world, to God. That said, most people cannot make that kind of confession – they are too stupid or too comfortable to take such crucial decisions.

For Kierkegaard, all individuals lead their lives in a situation that produces intolerable tension. They have to accept being transitory, finite creatures. At the same time, he believed, during their allotted span of life, human beings must accept that they are free. All this they must endure beneath a sky that suggests indifference despite being where God is to be found. Kierkegaard always kept faith with God, even though his books can be read as an introduction to an *existential philosophy*, which, in the final analysis, can manage perfectly well without any form of Almighty.

The same is true of the central argument in Kierkegaard's philosophy, the so-called theory of 'stages', in which the final stage, the 'religious' one, is probably the most crucial. The philosopher appears to be equally at home in the two previous stages of our journey through life, the 'aesthetic' and 'ethical' stages. He also seems to enjoy the middle ground of 'irony'.

Kierkegaard himself had a great gift for irony and, unlike people whom he considers capable of irony but not 'humour', Kierkegaard had a marvellous comic talent. It was as if quiet desperation – whose obverse, incidentally, is 'inexpressible joy' – had given Kierkegaard the talent to impale on his wit all the most ludicrous, affected and absurd qualities of human life. He did not exclude himself – and this was one of the most endearing of Kierkegaard's qualities as a philosopher – from his tendency to mock.

In 1843, when he was studying philosophy in Berlin and 'fell very ill out of sheer terror', he made the following note. 'Now I'm reasonably well . . . I'm walking with a stick . . . Otherwise, though, as I said, I'm pretty weak, my legs tremble, I get pains in my knees, and so on, it's not vivid enough, so I'll choose a phrase from my favourite actor, Mr Grobecker, an expression he brilliantly weaves into every fourth sentence: "I've fallen down and it's all over" – or, in a truly inspired variant: "I'm all over and it's fallen down" .'

The family album of philosophers who devised great systems gives pride of place to *Hegel,* whom Kierkegaard did not admire very much. Kierkegaard left philosophers who devised great philosophical systems – not least Hegel, whom he did not admire very much – with a rather sobering thought. Kierkegaard's own entry read as follows. 'Most architects of philosophical systems have the same attitude to those systems as someone who, having built an enormous castle, then decides to live in a nearby barn . . .'

'After breaking off his engagement in 1841, Kierkegaard went to Berlin where he attended Schelling's lectures . . .'
SW 315

Jean de Lamarck
....

Lamarck (1744–1829) is supposed to have coined the term 'biology'. He started life as an army officer and was later professor of zoology in Paris.

His theory of evolution – 'Lamarckism' – starts from the premise that changes in environment cause changes in an *organism* which can be inherited. The same applies to human beings. In his day, Lamarck's theory was immensely influential and had an impact on research by *Darwin*, among others.

'The idea of biological evolution began to be widely accepted in some circles as early as 1800. The leading spokesman for this idea was the French zoologist *Lamarck* . . .'
SW 339

Julien Offroy de La Mettrie

Although in his day what he said was fiercely rejected, now his thesis seems much more plausible and close to the truth: namely, that human beings are machines – not perfect, admittedly, but functioning by the billion.

All things considered, then, it seems as if we owe Monsieur La Mettrie (1709–51) an apology. Even those fellow thinkers – the moralists and socialists – who came after him spurned and scorned him. His teachings are enough to disillusion anyone permanently. According to La Mettrie, the mind – that overbearing organ – can work only if an intact body allows it to work. The same applies to the soul. What a person wants has nothing to do with the human being as such, only with the machine that keeps a person running – so long as it goes on working.

'The French physician and philosopher *La Mettrie* wrote a book in the eighteenth century called *L'homme machine*, which means "Man – the machine" . . .'
SW 192

Pierre Simon de Laplace

Laplace (1749–1827) was a mathematician, astronomer and philosopher. He was happiest when concerned with the planets, which, in his view, came into being in a violently rotating cloud of gas.

He became well known for the 'Laplace Daemon', an invented, theoretical figure that is familiar with all natural laws and forces, as well as the movements of minute particles. All in all, then, it knows about absolutely everything. This means that it could pronounce on events in a specific place at a specific time.

'Later on, the French mathematician *Laplace* expressed an extreme mechanistic view . . .'
SW 192

Gottfried Wilhelm Leibniz
....

It may well be true that the soul 'cannot even be divided into two'. Nor – so far as we know – has anyone ever seen the soul. Yet we cannot manage without it. That was certainly true for Leibniz, a polymath, who was so learned that his contemporaries, who could never quite match his learning, eventually lost respect for him and said many unkind things about him. Among the worst was the accusation that he did not make all his discoveries himself, but copied them from others.

Leibniz (1646–1716) responded with restrained bitterness. In no way did this slander alter his attitude to life, which was based on an absolutely positive view of the universe in its primal state – what he called its 'pre-established harmony'.

His father was a professor and the family took the child's precocious gifts in their stride – they were, after all, not ordinary people. After completing his studies, Leibniz was employed at court, first in Mainz, then in Hanover. He worked in the diplomatic service, which left him enough time to carry out intensive scientific research and to correspond with the leading intellects of Europe. Later, he worked as a Minister Without Portfolio, which also left him a great deal of free time.

Multi-talented, Leibniz completed almost all the tasks he was given to the satisfaction of his superiors. He concerned himself with mining and coinage, he was familiar with various aspects of the law, and he managed one of the largest libraries of his day as if he himself had written all the books it contained. Finally – much to the distress of subsequent generations of schoolchildren – he also invented differential and integral calculus (see *Newton*).

Central to Leibniz's philosophy is the doctrine of 'monads'. Monads – from the Greek *monas*, meaning 'unit' – are the primal substances out of which everything was created. They are the smallest possible units, and cannot be further subdivided. God, who created the 'best of all possible worlds', created them long ago and made them independent or, in Leibniz's words, 'self-existent', so that he did not need to trouble himself with them further. The phenomenon of time, Leibniz continued, does not apply to monads, which are thus imperishable. Because of their 'indivisibility', they do not occupy space, either.

Monads can join together and form 'aggregates'. However, as 'self-existent' units, they are concerned only with themselves – or, as a famous sentence of Leibniz's puts it, 'monads have no windows'. That said, they are accorded a reflective function. They 'mirror' the world, and their infinite diversity ensures that innumerable different worlds are reflected in the various monad-mirrors.

Leibniz allows for higher, more complex forms of knowledge by drawing a fundamental distinction between simple monads that form matter, and those that make up the soul. These, Leibniz believes, are capable of 'apperception', a process of perception that enables them to be aware of themselves, and which includes the abilities to think, feel and remember.

Leibniz sought to devise a philosophy that would constitute a universal science with a clear conscience. Truly miraculous things were expected of a *rational* science of this kind. People believed it capable of a great deal – of anything at all, in fact – and were in no mood to be disappointed.

'An important seventeenth century philosopher named *Leibniz* pointed out that the difference between the material and the spiritual is precisely that the material can be broken up into smaller and smaller bits, but the soul cannot even be divided into two . . .'
SW 193

Lenin

Marxism was developed so fully by the people committed to its realization that it finally bore little resemblance to its original form. The view is more a criticism of the people responsible for the development than the philosophy that they distorted for their own purposes. In the now distant days when an authoritarian form of State Socialism made its appearance under the guise of Communism, leading politicians often imagined they were also expected to be leading intellectuals.

One of them was Vladimir Ilich Ulyanov (1870–1924), who was later – when he became the leader and triumphant victor of the Russian Revolution – known as Lenin. From his time at grammar school onwards, he concerned himself mainly with the theory of knowledge because, in his opinion, correct knowledge had a direct bearing on correct practice. Exaggerated doubts were not something from which Lenin suffered. As he said, 'Social consciousness reflects social realities.' Views like this were nothing if not political.

Lenin will probably not be remembered much for his philosophy. Even so, he said something very pertinent about the Germans. If, he alleged, they were ever to have a revolution that involved commandeering a railway station, they would buy a platform ticket first. Even allowing for the fact that these days you don't need a platform ticket to get into a station, the anecdote aptly sums up the German character.

'In our own century, Lenin, Stalin, Mao and many others also made their contribution to Marxism, or Marxism-Leninism . . .'
SW 326

Leonardo da Vinci

The illustrious Italian painter, sculptor and architect was also a gifted natural scientist and loved puzzles. Leonardo (1452–1519) restored the theoretical outline of the natural sciences to favour.

In his imagination he constructed the first aeroplanes and submarines. The drawings of these, which he completed himself, make the machines look not only fantastic, but also exceptionally realistic. Leonardo believed in the possibility of an encyclopaedic knowledge based on experiment and sensory perception – and capable ultimately of rising to abstract heights.

'But Luther was not a humanist like Ficino or *Leonardo da Vinci* . . .'
SW 178

John Locke
....

Apparently, as soon as they know something, many people want to know everything. The philosopher John Locke (1632–1704) always wanted to know everything. This is why he pursued philosophy only as a sideline, also applying himself to viniculture, public finance, theology, economics, jurisprudence, geography and mathematics, as well as medicine. He was also active as a politician, civil servant, teacher and family doctor. On top of all this, he was reputedly rather good at tennis.

Locke founded British *empiricism*. One of his key theses was that nothing could find its way into the mind which had not first passed through the senses. He compares a child's rationality, which at first is more like irrationality, to blank 'white paper', on which the world waits to be recorded – a task for which one generally has a whole lifetime. According to Locke, 'the materials of reason and knowledge' come from 'experience'. The same applies to *consciousness* of oneself, which results from a learning process. It is also true of ideas, the 'complex' forms of which arise from 'comparing' and 'abstracting' what Locke calls 'simple ideas'.

Locke also stresses that we should not underestimate the role of language. This forms 'sense data' or 'ideas of sensation', and has an indispensably creative function within the mind's thinking processes when it wishes to communicate something 'meaningful'. Locke's distinction between 'primary' qualities, such as solidity, number, shape and position, and 'secondary' ones, including tastes and colours, was certainly a significant – albeit controversial – contribution to the basis of knowledge.

This discussion was taken further, and eventually – outside the British Isles – adopted by *idealist* philosophy, which came to entirely different conclusions. This did not necessarily invalidate Locke. Even though he liked to appear as rather a pessimist among philosophers, he found most of his ideas confirmed in his lifetime. Empiricism was a strong philosophical suit, and the rich supply of experience flowing in from the outside world every day appeared to confirm him in his beliefs. Despite the self-restraint he recommended, Locke still had a profound sense of beauty and timeless values.

His political philosophy is liberal, thrifty and market oriented. As the supreme social regulator, *reason* shows its individual character in the right to own property – one that is common to all citizens. That said, citizens' property rights are synonymous with the property they actually own. Anyone not owning much cannot have acted in a very rational way and should therefore be content with fewer rights. This is at least an honest viewpoint, which – perhaps not openly – is still espoused by many a property-owner nowadays.

'Locke . . . the mind is as bare and empty as a blackboard before the teacher arrives in the classroom . . .'
SW 218

Logos

....

In Greek philosophy, logos denotes a principle of *reason* to which creative powers are attributed. In *Heraclitus*'s work, logos means the 'law governing the world', for *Aristotle* it has to do with the meaning of rational definitions, and philosophers of the *Stoa* personalized it, putting it on a par with the divine soul of the world. Finally, Christianity – especially St John's Gospel – equated the logos with the word of God, which is made flesh in Jesus Christ, the son of Man and of God.

'Instead of the term "God", Heraclitus often used the Greek word *logos* . . .'
SW 31

Martin Luther

Luther (1483–1546) was not merely a theologian, a controversial reformer and a Bible translator of genius, but also a philosopher, who valued his own philosophical abilities highly. The quality he found most appealing about philosophy was the art of resolving contradictions. In fact, he jealously guarded his *dialectical* skills because human beings themselves have to come to terms with the greatest contradiction of all – their freedom as Christians. This may well stand firm 'among ordinary things', as Luther puts it, but it can look very feeble in the sight of God. Faced with their Creator, human beings are reduced to silence – they are, after all, merely creatures. To illustrate his point, Luther offers a striking image: a human being, he suggests, can be compared to a horse which is ridden by either God or the Devil.

As well as embellishing his Bible translation with several brilliantly expressive verbal jewels, Luther is credited with some trenchant insights. One of them runs: 'The essence of language is the chance it gives us to be heard.' And to describe our existence on earth he made a very pithy remark that makes a lot of novels and jeremiads seem superfluous: 'We are beggars. That is God's truth.'

'Yes, *Martin Luther* was important, but he was not the only reformer . . .'
SW 177

Thomas Malthus

Malthus (1766–1834) was initially a clergyman, then a professor of history and political economy. He swiftly rose to be an expert on population when, at an early date, he wrote two essays protesting against unchecked growth in the numbers of human beings, who, he maintained, could not produce enough food for the extra mouths that they created. This view, which Malthus rather resignedly linked with an appeal for more self-restraint in controlling appetites, strikes us as highly appropriate to conditions nowadays.

It will surprise no one to learn that as a philosopher Malthus was pessimistic. Among several more gloomy reflections, he also turned his thoughts to wars and plagues, which, he believed, might have a 'beneficial' effect on alarming population statistics.

'. . . he {Darwin} chanced to come across a little book by the specialist in population studies, *Thomas Malthus . . .*'
SW 343

Manichaeism

Named after the doctrine taught by the Persian, Mani (*c.*216–*c.*276), Manichaeism was a successful religion, especially in the fourth century. It combined Christian convictions with elements of Persian religion.

St Augustine, the father of the Church, was an active Manichaean, and remained one for around ten years, before he identified strongly with the Christian Church. Later, as a high Church dignitary, he doggedly kept repeating: 'I know what I'm saying!' and condemned his erstwhile fellow-believers as intransigent heretics.

Manichaeism is structured in a radically dualistic way. It sees the world divided into two co-eternal principles – good and evil – which are fundamentally equal in importance. Other opposites, such as light and darkness, body and soul, life and death, can be included. Human beings must choose – and go on choosing all their lives. This appears to accord them a degree of free will that later Christianity did not really envisage.

'The Manichaeans were a religious sect that was extremely characteristic of late antiquity . . .'
SW 146

Mao Zedong

In earlier times, when people acted in a friendly – if not reverent – way towards him, the name Mao Zedong (1893–1976) was Mao Tse-tung. The same fate has befallen him that befell *Lenin* and *Stalin*: namely, that history has declared him *persona non grata*.

Like *Lenin* and *Stalin*, Mao, the erstwhile 'great helmsman' of the Chinese Revolution, was also a philosopher – or at least regarded himself as one. This should come as no surprise, for, according to the once honourable ideology of Communism, anyone could and should do everything. Someone who was a fisherman, hunter, worker and Party functionary might as well be a philosopher – or a poet and thinker, too.

As a philosopher, Mao wrote one of the most successful works in the history of philosophy, the *Little Red Book*. This is a collection of aphoristic sayings, interspersed with combative exhortations, which helped to enthuse the masses who at that time wanted change.

The *Little Red Book* contains a great many sayings that would not be out of place in management seminars. They include advice like: 'In all situations you have to exercise your intellect and think hard', which is tantamount to saying: 'Our thinking has to adapt to changed circumstances.'

'In our own century, Lenin, Stalin, Mao and many others also made their contribution to Marxism, or Marxism-Leninism . . .'
SW 326

Marcus Aurelius
. . . .

As a philosopher-king, he fulfilled *Plato*'s wish that all the philosophers who had been trained in his philosophy should be gifted enough to be rulers. As a politician, Marcus Aurelius (121–80) was unlucky.

This was due to circumstances rather than any political failings on his part. The Roman Empire was breaking up, and rebellion was the order of the day. The Emperor was obliged to move from one bivouac to another, where he valiantly continued writing his *Meditations*.

In his philosophy, Marcus Aurelius was influenced by *Stoic* philosophers, whose innate conscientiousness and moral seriousness he much appreciated. Later on, however, he began to have doubts. His very moderate *rational* optimism collapsed, and his own individually cultivated skills of self-discipline failed to work effectively. In his work, he began to sound a more sombre note, as in: 'Everything physical is in flux, everything spiritual is dream and delusion, life itself is a war when one is encamped far from home . . .'.

'. . . and many of them {the Stoics} , notably the Roman Emperor *Marcus Aurelius* (AD 121–180), were active statesmen . . .'
SW 110–11

Karl Marx

. . . .

Karl Marx (1818–83) is regarded as the only philosopher who succeeded in making philosophy a practical reality. An entire movement – Marxism – was named after him (SW 320ff.). The movements connected with it – Socialism or Social Democracy (SW 333) and Communism (SW 331) – were successful for a long time. By now, however, Social Democracy is more or less out of fashion, and Communism has almost completely disappeared.

Born the son of a lawyer, Marx was meant to follow in his father's footsteps and study law, which he duly did – though under protest. He was more interested in philosophy, especially *Hegel*, who, although dead by then, was still very influential. Hegel's pupils, who held several chairs at German universities, made sure he remained in vogue.

What most interested Marx about Hegel was his *dialectics* and the self-motivation of the human mind or spirit. Marx felt that neither had yet been properly understood, let alone tested against reality. Meanwhile, this reality was worsening noticeably. The working population was getting poorer all the time, while wealth continued to accumulate in the pockets of a few 'capitalists'. The Industrial Revolution dominated production, with the result that more and more key elements of the manufacturing process were taken over by machines, leading to large-scale unemployment.

Massive impoverishment appeared to be on the horizon. This looked like being all the more appalling as it went hand in hand with dramatic economic improvements. These included rising production and increasing capitalist power as manufacturing potential expanded. In this situation, Marx, who had by now gained his doctorate in philosophy, stood Hegel 'on his head'. In other words, he made him 'materialistic' – disencumbering him, as Marx believed, from his emphasis on the intellect, and giving his insights a practical application to everyday life.

Marx believed it was high time human beings were accorded the dignity of labour, and liberated from oppression and 'alienation'. He also thought that philosophy should be brought 'down to earth from heaven'. There, on earth, Marx continued, philosophy teaches us 'that for other human beings, a human being is the most advanced creature of all'. Further, he continued, philosophy demands the 'overthrow of all conditions under which human beings are humiliated, enslaved, abandoned, and despised'.

After completing his studies, Marx worked as a journalist. He found a friend and fellow-campaigner in Friedrich Engels (1820–95), an entrepreneur's son who had been attracted to Socialism at an early age. Engels often helped Marx out of his chronic financial difficulties. The two friends were a writing team who provided the Labour Movement – on an international as well as a national level – with the theories it could implement in practice.

After the 1848 Revolution, Marx and his family moved from Germany to England, where he spent the rest of his life. Engels, meanwhile, stayed in his father's firm, 'doggedly serving commerce', and went on earning the money to finance his friend and the Movement. Meanwhile, after intensively studying economics and politics, Marx had developed a philosophy of history. This sounded extremely appealing as it suggested a way out of hopeless poverty.

One of its key theses goes like this: 'It is not human beings' *consciousness* which determines their reality, but – on the contrary – it is their social reality which determines their consciousness. At a certain stage of their development, the productive forces of society come into conflict with the prevailing conditions of production – or, and this is only a legal way of saying the same thing – with the conditions of ownership within which they have hitherto operated. These conditions change from developed forms of productive forces into constraints limiting that development. Then a period of social revolution sets in.'

Marx and Engels firmly believed that this revolution was just around the corner. Capitalism, they thought, would be forced to expand to the very limit, and thus create the conditions for its own downfall. This, they believed, would be accomplished by the very people whom capitalism had oppressed for so long. As we know, Marx and Engels did not live to see the revolution they so ardently desired. It came later and, as we have mentioned earlier, it did not take place in one of the highly developed industrialized countries in the West, but in Russia, which was far less developed.

At first, this historical delay did not lessen the impact of Marxist philosophy. People believed Marxists when they said: 'Philosophers have only managed to interpret the world in different ways – what matters now is to change that world.' That said, the changes which then occurred failed to fulfil philosophers' expectations. Human consciousness, it appeared, was less than happy with the subordinate role into which it was now cast.

In Hegel's philosophy, consciousness had still been a main player. Now, after Marx, it was allowed to respond only to cues from the wings – it was to be nothing more than a knee-jerk reaction to social conditions. The problem of Marx's philosophy was not the fact that it failed to achieve its morally honourable goal of social justice. Its real problem was its unrealistic one-sidedness. It appropriated the truth so obsessively that it could brook no argument. At the same time, it still believed it had discovered the laws governing the world and history – and even the outlines of the future.

'Marx . . . a spectre is haunting Europe . . .'
SW 320

Materialism

Like its tried and tested counterpart, *idealism*, materialism is a time-honoured philosophical trend – perhaps even more old-established, for it is based on a realistic assessment of things. In the past, rather more abstract forms of knowledge, which are rightly proud of their achievements in the field of consciousness, must have also started from the same point. Without basing ourselves fully on the facts of our physical existence – so the argument runs – it is impossible to make any significant discoveries about consciousness or to explore our mentality.

Materialism has always played a slightly provocative part in the history of philosophy. Its role has been to blow some fresh air into firmly fixed debates. Anyone who listens to a trained materialist explaining the world may well breathe a sigh of relief – in that things don't have to be so intricate, complex or cranky as we might have feared. That said, there are some natural truths that no one can deny.

Materialistic arguments, which early philosophers, such as *Democritus* and *Epicurus*, introduced, have worked best when free of proscriptive detail, such as the so-called dialectical materialism first developed by *Marx*.

Denis Diderot (1713–84) – a philosopher of genius – shows that materialistic philosophy can also have its moments of day-dreaming, reflection and even godliness. He described what it can mean to know you have been elevated into the sphere of the nameless 'Other', the sum total of all things natural. As he himself says: 'It exists, and we exist. Everything is useful, everything is helpful, and has a contribution to make . . . The individual is nothing without trying to be something . . . Stay still, stay still, stay like everything around you, let the hours, and days and years just drift past like everything around you, and fade away like everything around you . . .'

'We should just mention a final current, *materialism* . . .'
SW 383

Middle Ages

The period of the Middle Ages covers quite a long span of time. It reaches from the fifth to the early sixteenth centuries. This extended span needs breaking up further. Accordingly, we talk in terms of the Early Middle Ages – from the fifth to the tenth centuries; the High Middle Ages – from the eleventh to the thirteenth centuries; and the Late Middle Ages – the mid-thirteenth century to the early sixteenth century.

For a long time people held the *Enlightenment* view that medieval times were the 'Dark Ages'. This prejudice even became proverbial for a while. Then, a gradual shift in opinion began to take place.

Today we know that not everything about the Middle Ages was dark. In the High Middle Ages, for example, 'real love' was reputedly first discovered, and this is an ideal to which we still aspire, perhaps against our better judgement.

'The Middle Ages . . . going only part of the way is not the same as going the wrong way . . .'
SW 138

John Stuart Mill

Mill (1806–73) was a writer, economist, philosopher and Member of Parliament. For 35 years he also worked in the Examiner's Office of the East India Company, where he himself maintained he could engage in 'the real study of the world.'

As a philosopher, Mill continued the tradition of British *empiricism*. For him, knowledge is 'a posteriori', grounded in experience, although this cannot be trusted in all cases. The same is even more true of 'sensation', which prepares the ground for experience. All perceptions need to be constantly tested and confirmed afresh.

Towards the end of his career, Mill was regarded as a decisive campaigner for total equality between men and women. His book, *The Subjection of Women*, which appeared in German under the rather misleading title of *The Enslavement of Woman* (*Die Hörigkeit der Frau*) – is now considered a classic of women's literature.

'He {Locke} had a great influence on *John Stuart Mill*, who in turn had a key role in the struggle for equality of the sexes . . .'
SW 220

Mode

···

A 'mode' – from the Latin *modus*, meaning 'way, measure or rule' – denotes a way of being, a condition or, by extension, a quality that is a prerequisite for an object's form of existence.

For us human beings, who have difficulty relating to one another, the *modus vivendi* has taken pride of place. In order to achieve this, we need to find the *modus procendi*, the appropriate method of proceeding.

'A "mode" is the particular manner which Substance, God or nature assumes . . .'
SW 208

Monism

Monism takes the view that the world and everything in it consists of one uniform basic substance. This substance can be God himself or a form of *consciousness* determining everything, a life-giving force that flows through the whole universe – or, to quote *Heraclitus*, a 'world-law'. That said, it is also possible – as the work of some early Greek philosophers shows – to specify a form of matter that is responsible for the creation and operation of everything that exists.

If, within monism, we think in terms of an omnipresent God, then we talk about *monotheism* (SW 128). Judaism and Islam are strictly monotheistic religions. That said, Christianity, which also believes in only one God, applies monism in a slightly more sophisticated way. It prefers to think in terms of a 'trinity', the sacred triune of God the Father, the Son and the Holy Ghost.

'There is only one nature, they {the Stoics} averred. This kind of idea is called *monism . . .*'
SW 110

Charles Montesquieu

Montesquieu (1689–1755), the jurist and legal philosopher, was a legend in his own lifetime. He became famous for his industry and feared for his learning. His library was like a labyrinth, and on top of everything else, he reputedly invented the card-index box.

Montesquieu campaigned for the rights of the nobility, to which he belonged. Without the nobility to balance out extremes, he maintained, the state would deteriorate into either an 'Oriental tyranny' or 'mob rule' – by which he meant democracy. As a philosopher, he was one of the earliest sociologists. He studied the mechanics of constitutional and legal systems, working on the assumption that from a scientific standpoint it made no difference whether one was studying natural processes or institutions that human beings had called into being.

Montesquieu's notion of the division of power – into the legislative, executive and judiciary – has been embodied in almost all the constitutional forms adopted by the type of state about which he had so many doubts – democracy.

'This division of power originated from the French Fnlightenment philosopher *Montesquieu . . .'*
SW 221

Muhammad

Muhammad (570–632), the founder of Islam, whose Arabic name means 'the Praised One', was originally a respected merchant. In that capacity, he undertook journeys during which he familiarized himself with Christianity, Judaism and other religions.

In 610, he was visited by visions, and he felt summoned to be a prophet. He proclaimed his teachings in Mecca, where they not only found followers, but were written down in a binding form in the Koran – the Word of God.

In Islam, which in Arabic means 'submission to God's will', Muhammad's position as a prophet and ambassador of the one and only God – Allah – is an incontrovertible fact that has achieved the force of law.

'After the death of Muhammad . . . both the Middle East and North Africa were won over to Islam . . .'
SW 145

Mysticism

The notion of mysticism comes from the Greek word *myein*, which means something like 'closing the eyes'. This gives us some indication of where mystics' experience takes place – in the head, behind closed eyes. They are attempting to return to the depths of their soul, to achieve insight into their inner essence. By this, mystics do not generally mean the self. They are, however, striving towards the ultimate form of unity, union with God – as in the Latin phrase: *unio mystica*.

In mysticism, which is at least as old as philosophy, we can hear echoes of ancient human longings, as well as fear of being inadequate and anxieties triggered by the transience of creation. There have been mystical movements at all periods, in all cultures.

Nowadays, we believe that mystical experiences – especially those focusing on self-discovery – can be learnt and communicated. This is why experts in self-discovery – people who have looked for and found themselves – offer courses and books based on techniques of meditation and ecstasy, as well as highly enticing journeys to the very centre of the human pysche.

'In *Western mysticism* – that is, within Judaism, Christianity, and Islam – the mystic emphasizes that his meeting is with a personal God . . .'
SW 116

Myth

. . . .

There is not much to say except that myth – from the Greek, meaning 'word, poetic story' – does not have to be a story about gods. It can also tell of other long-past events that are revived in fantastic or symbolic narrative, thus arousing fresh interest.

A myth recreates primordial times, incidents which – in whatever form – have shaped things that happened subsequently. To this extent, myths also indicate paths, and leave pointers that lead into the present day. A cautious approach, coupled with an unbiased ability to question and listen, is needed to work out what myths, all of which tend to take enigmatic, intricate forms, might actually mean.

'A myth is a story about the gods which sets out to explain why life is as it is . . .'
SW 19

Natural right

A natural right is an original right. It is not created by human convention or statute. This, however, is the start of its problems. A right that is derived from *nature*, which does not acknowledge any rights at all – or, at most, only the rights of the strongest and best adapted – is bound to remain vague.

All in all, then, a natural right has more to do with original thinking, the kind that appeals to human *reason* – which optimists believe is available to everyone. The problems that the notion of natural right causes are built into its structure. These are exacerbated whenever individual questions have to be resolved on the basis of a right expressed in very general terms.

An example is whether or not the death penalty is justified by natural right. This question, which is now once more a burning issue in the USA, was hotly debated in the discussions of natural rights that took place in the seventeenth century.

'For instance, he {Descartes} held that certain ethical principles applied to everyone. In other words, he believed in the idea of a *natural right* . . .'
SW 220

Nature

Fundamentally, the notion of nature has a twofold meaning. First, the word means original essence – the special quality of something lies in the *nature* of what it is. Secondly, nature signifies all-encompassing wholeness, the *natural* context of the world, including everything about it that is independent of human beings – as in Goethe's phrase: 'Nature is everything.'

Initially, human beings felt part of nature and understood they were creatures living among other creatures. Later, though, they discovered their ostensible difference in kind. Their *consciousness* began to play an active role; as did their mind or spirit – which *Hegel*, in particular, built up into something inimical to nature. Finally, culture began to signify the sum total of special human achievements, and was free of any necessity for natural survival.

Human beings have certainly distanced themselves from nature in her original form. It appears to be part of their nature not to be able to cope any longer with how nature used to be. Instead, they have for a long time now posed as engineers of nature. They use her, abuse her, exploit her for their own ends, make her artificial and change her radically – without ever reflecting that in the past nature got on perfectly well without them and will in the future do so again. That said, the reverse does not apply, for human beings need nature in order to stay alive.

Philosophy itself has not helped here. Philosophers must share the blame for our having lost our innate humility towards nature, replacing it with a form of possessiveness. This makes human beings appear to be the lords of creation, who must always be provided with what is apparently theirs. The philosophy of Marxism-Leninism has exaggerated this possessive attitude, but it was prepared for in Hegelian *idealism*, where nature is seen as a desolate halfway house on the way to the spirit.

In the wake of their attempts to find themselves – which often verge on the comic or even desperate – people nowadays are again searching for their 'inner nature', for those mysterious sources of motivation deep inside them that make them what they are.

But what, we might ask, are they if they cannot or will not be natural creatures any longer; if their 'second nature' – their socially, historically, culturally conditioned patterns of behaviour – has also become suspect?

'If she had grown up in this garden without knowing anything at all about nature, how would she feel about the spring? . . .'
SW 24

Isaac Newton
....

This great universal scholar had objectives that were far clearer than the many complicated accounts he presented to his often slow-witted contemporaries. One was his declared intention to foster science by studying exact evidence in *nature*.

For his philosophical programme, Newton (1642–1727) dispensed with rational principles that were independent of experience. Stating boldly that he was not going to invent 'hypotheses', he believed that experiments were their own justification, and that they brought to light the results already latent within them. Accordingly, he believed that clever theories are of secondary importance – they are necessary only when facts have already been communicated. What matters most, Newton felt, was well-informed research into the object under scrutiny.

Newton made key discoveries in natural science, establishing theoretical mechanics, formulating the law of gravitation and making a significant contribution to the science of optics. He 'invented' or 'discovered' differential calculus at the same time as *Leibniz*, and this led to a dispute over copyright, conducted largely by the two men's pupils. Newton's theory of light made him unpopular with Goethe, who had developed his own 'Theory of Colours' ('Farbenlehre'), which he considered more astute and, above all, more accurate than the work undertaken by the scientist whom Goethe called 'this Newton'.

'Yes, along came Newton. He formulated what we call the *Law of Universal Gravitation* . . .'
SW 174

Friedrich Nietzsche

Nietzsche (1844–1900) gave philosophy a fascination it had not previously had. This was principally because Nietzsche was at least as much a creative writer as he was a philosopher. He wrote brilliant prose, in which he was able to express all the nuances of his experiences of the world and of himself.

Another reason for Nietzsche's fame is the fact that he lived his philosophy as if it were his life. He learnt to recognize all the states, visions and anxieties – as well as the anger and arrogance – that he lugged around with him. Out of this rich brew he concocted philosophical insights that sound sometimes true, sometimes exaggerated, sometimes magnificent and sometimes small-minded.

Superficially, Nietzsche's life has some qualities of Christ's Passion. He started out as a young genius, becoming a professor of classical philology in Basle at the age of 24. He was then forced to take early retirement for health reasons. Subsequently, he was never free of this illness, which culminated in insanity – though experts are still divided about both the illness and the insanity. After his early retirement, Nietzsche led an unstable life with lots of travel, in which phases of euphoric clear-sightedness alternated with periods of deep depression. His philosophy developed without any major stimuli from the outside world. This gives it great suggestive power, and imbues it with a suggestion of direct experience normally absent from academic philosophical discussions.

Nietzsche's philosophy picks its way along a hilly path of his own choosing, which, in the final analysis, leads past nothing but chasms. The philosopher gives himself heart along the way. He invests his metaphysical world with new energy by making it radical and anti-human, even though in private life he remained an appealingly modest, withdrawn, sometimes even shy man. Thus, all those things he can never be are fashioned into the 'Superman'. Nietzsche believes that this figure, who is unmoved by anything, is destined to rule the future world. He becomes infatuated with the 'will to power', and never tires of elaborating his favourite idea – the 'eternal recurrence of the same thing'.

In describing the notion of eternal recurrence, Nietzsche reaches the heights of poetic expression. 'And do you know what the world is to me? Shall I show it to you in my mirror? This world: a monstrous power, which does not grow larger, or smaller, which is never exhausted but merely changes, remaining the same size the whole time, a household without expenses or losses, but at the same time without growth, without income, surrounded by a "void" as if by a frontier; nothing is blurred, spent or infinitely extended – everything is located in a special space as a special power . . . a sea of stormily churning and rushing forces, never pausing, transforming themselves, coiling back on themselves, over timeless aeons of recurrence, its figures ebbing and flowing, swirling away from the simplest to the most complex, from the stillest, stiffest, coldest to the most fiery, savage and self-contradictory, then retreating once again from fullness to simplicity, from an interplay of inconsistencies to the happiness of harmony, reaffirming themselves in the certainty of their fixed orbits and their years, blessing one another as the essence of things that will eternally recur . . .'

'Another important philosopher who had a great influence on the twentieth century was the German *Friedrich Nietzsche* . . .'
SW 377

Nihilism

The term comes from *nihil*, the Latin for 'nothing'. As a philosophy, it stands for a view of the world in which nothing can be satisfactory. Nihilists are chronically weary because they can see through everything, they have understood everything and they draw one main conclusion from it all. This is that life is not worth the candle, since all the grand expectations, hopes and dreams people invest in it are just mirages on the horizon. Looking more closely, they argue, one simply sees what was there to start with – namely, nothing.

The German philosopher Jacobi (1743–1819) introduced the notion of nihilism into philosophy, partly as a criticism of his colleague, Fichte. Later on, nihilism became well known through the novel *Fathers and Sons*, by the Russian writer Turgenev.

Nietzsche identified one reason for nihilistic thinking – the fact that human beings have been robbed of their own significance. As he says, 'Since Copernicus, people seem to have been stumbling down a slippery slope – now they are tumbling faster and faster away from the centre – where to? into the void? into an excruciating sense of their own nothingness?'

'Although Sartre claimed there was no innate meaning to life, he did not mean that nothing mattered. He was not what we call a *nihilist* . . .'
SW 380

Novalis

Novalis's real name was Friedrich von Hardenberg. As a *Romantic* poet, however, he used a pseudonym, which means something like 'tiller of fresh soil'. Novalis (1772–1801) was a philosopher as well as a creative writer. He saw no real difference between them, as both literature and philosophy gave him the 'one key' to his 'innermost self'. Like *Nietzsche*, he had that rare ability to write about unique insights in a unique way. Also like *Nietzsche*, he matured early as an artist and concentrated the experience of a whole lifetime into just a few years.

He understood the other-worldliness of the real world, the permanence within transience and, ultimately, the egocentricity of the ego, as well as the humanness of being human. 'Perception,' he wrote, 'is a universal state which is not limited to one specific instance . . . Our ego's accidental or specific form ceases only as a specific form, in other words, death is the end only of egotism . . . The element of accident must fade away, whilst the quality of goodness must remain, for it forms part of the whole. This wholeness is present in every moment, every phenomenon. Humankind and the eternal are ever-present . . .'

This vision of the world blurs traditional borderlines – including those between waking and dreaming. But it is an attitude fraught with danger – for instance, the danger that we will lose so much touch with reality that the fine arts cannot pull us back. Even so, Novalis always believed in the creative power of dreams, which, he maintained, help stabilize reality more firmly.

Novalis also believed that dreams help to prevent knowledge being focused exclusively on the real world. Instead, he argued, they shift us towards an inner sphere where our heart, soul and ultimate human worth are to be found. 'We dream about voyaging through the cosmos – but is the cosmos not within us? Veiled in mystery, our path leads deep inside us. All the worlds of eternity – the past as well as the future – are either within us or do not exist at all . . . The first genius to burst through his own boundaries found the characteristic germ of his own immeasurable universe within . . . At any moment any human being is capable of being a supra-sensory creature. Without this capability he or she would be an animal rather than a citizen of the world.'

'*Novalis*, one of the young geniuses {of Romanticism} , said that: "the world becomes a dream, and the dream becomes reality" . . .'
SW 288

Organism

. . . .

The term comes from the Greek *organon*, meaning 'implement', and at first it meant the material unity of a living creature in its unique particularly.

In any organism, which always takes on a form that is typical of its individuality and is visible from the outside, organs and other parts work together to make up a functioning whole. An organism is bound up with its environment by means of a continuous process of interchange, known as metabolism.

The term 'organism' was later also applied to other areas, which can sometimes lead to a certain arbitrariness.

'The Romantics considered both a plant and a nation to be a living organism. A poetic work was also a living organism . . .'
SW 292

Pantheism

The basic premise of pantheism is that God cannot be separated from his Creation. Philosophically, he is identified with the universe, with *nature* and also with human beings who have made themselves at home in his Creation.

If, however, everything is in God, then we might ask whether in the final analysis God is everything and thus no longer God. A phrase of Schopenhauer's may well be apposite here: 'Pantheism is the acceptable face of atheism.'

'Many held the view that God was also present in his creation . . . This idea is called *pantheism* . . .'
SW 168

Parmenides

Parmenides (*c.*515–*c.*450 BC) came from the Greek colony of Elea in southern Italy, which at that time was fertile soil for philosophers. The Eleatic School, founded by Parmenides and continued by his pupils, *Zeno* and *Melissus*, presents reality as a closed entity whose essential qualities become clear when thought through.

We know very little about Parmenides. That said, some works attributed to him have survived – such as longish passages from his major didactic poem, 'On Nature', which describes the path to enlightenment as a journey towards truth.

The poem begins with a prologue. A horse-drawn chariot takes Parmenides along the 'road rich in knowledge' up to the sun, where a goddess tells him first about 'real truth', then about the 'unreliable opinions' held by human beings on earth. The latter believe in what they see. They are constantly being deceived by their senses. They perceive opposites – in other words, contradictions – which they regard as reality, such as light and dark, motion and rest. From all this they conclude that contradictory phenomena can co-exist side by side.

However, the 'real truth' is that everything which is exists only in itself – an entity that is entirely undifferentiated and completely timeless. 'Neither was it once, nor will it ever be, for it is now, at once entire, one, complete in itself.'

Parmenides bases this less than blinding revelation on a process of thought. He writes: 'This is thinking and an object of thought', and as such is always directed at something that exists. To think of something that 'is not' is, for Parmenides, tantamount to not thinking – and, by extension therefore, to not existing.

The real charm of this philosophy, which also influenced later thinkers, including Plato, Hegel and Nietzsche, lies in its splendidly stubborn effort to establish, by means of thought, a counter-balancing force in the path of reality, hurtling by at break-neck speed – in other words, to build a defensive wall as the tide rushes in.

Further, it is the tone of a visionary and prophet that endows Parmenides' writings with a quality of poetic truth, as in the passage: 'For there is nothing apart from what exists, and there never will be anything else; for destiny has decreed that it will be entire and immovable. Thus, everything is a series of hollow names, even though mortals have used language to assign these names to things in the belief that the things had some kind of reality, as in: "creation", "dissolution", "being" and "not-being", "changing places" and "shift of radiant colour".'

Parmenides thought that everything that exists had always existed . . .'
SW 29-30

St Paul, the Apostle

On the way to Damascus, Saul, the persecutor of Christians, was supposedly overcome by a vision, in which *Jesus Christ* revealed himself to him. In the Acts of the Apostles, we can read three different accounts of this event. Saul becomes Paul, and the erstwhile pursuer of Christians develops into one of their most eloquent preachers.

St Paul (*c.*10–*c.*67), an educated Jewish theologian who knew all the ins and outs of his former faith, opted for the radically alternative side of Christianity. This does not slavishly follow the Old Testament route of blind obedience to the Law, but boldly attempts to strike out along the new path indicated by Christ. He, St Paul writes: the 'first of those who fell asleep', 'loved me [St Paul] and sacrificed himself for me'. Then, St Paul continues, he was resurrected in order to lead human beings into the only worthwhile relationship with God – one that promises salvation.

As St Paul interprets the Christian story, the earlier verdict of damnation, pronounced by the severe Father, is later rescinded, because the Son has brought about reconciliation. This message demands absolute *faith*, for only someone who can unconditionally accept the mercy of God that Christ brings is also worthy of that mercy.

St Paul did a great deal to spread Christianity. His rhetorical skills impressed believers and unbelievers alike – an achievement that can be explained by the poetic vividness of his language. 'Put everything to the test and keep the best,' he reputedly said. The same applies to this independent philosopher's dealings with philosophical history.

'Many hundreds of years later, St Paul the Apostle stood here and preached about Jesus and Christianity to the Athenians . . .'
SW 64

Plato

. . . .

The philosopher Plato (427–347 BC) expressed his thanks to his teacher, the philosopher *Socrates*, in a very special way. He made him into a literary figure he could hide behind. Thus, some of the wisdom we attribute to Socrates probably belongs to Plato. In other words, Plato was the beneficiary of the philosophical legacy he himself bequeathed.

Plato came from an aristocratic family, and there is a lingering aristocratic quality about his philosophy, which offers very little to ordinary people – though a great deal to a philosophically literate élite. His first meeting with Socrates reputedly took place in 407. One of the chroniclers of philosophical history in those days lost no time in embellishing this encounter, as follows. 'There is a story that Socrates had a dream in which he had a young swan on his lap, which immediately grew feathers, ready for flight. Accordingly, it climbed into the sky with wild whoops of joy, and a day later Socrates was introduced to Plato whereupon he said that this was the bird he had seen in his dream . . .'

In his early days, Plato, here identified with the swan, was certainly free as a bird. He had tried his hand at poetry, and produced some fine verse of great profundity, such as: 'Look up to the other stars, my star. Oh, if only my thousand eyes were/ the sky itself, then I would look down upon you with them.'

Socrates, who cultivated an informal, conversational style, now instructed his favourite pupil in the serious art of profound thought. As a result, Plato changed his free-wheeling way of life and travelled widely, to extend his knowledge. In 387 he went to Sicily, where he entered the political arena, and worked as an adviser at the court of the tyrant King Dionysius I of Syracuse. Plato's attempts to give the rulers a little philosophical polish were not very successful. He returned to Athens and established his own philosophical school there. This was known as the Academy, and he was actively involved with it for almost 40 years.

Among several important pupils, his most famous one was

probably *Aristotle*, though the latter did not become his successor. Plato interrupted the tranquil harmony of his philosophical learning and teaching only twice more. He was seized by a spirit of adventure, and probably also by curiosity as to whether he could make politicians better politicians by first training them to be good philosophers. To put this to a practical test, he went back to Syracuse and tried to exercise a positive influence on the tyrant's son, Dionysius II, and his brother-in-law, Dion. This mission was an almost total disaster, too. Thus, Plato was forced to concentrate entirely on theory, which henceforth he pursued almost fanatically.

Those of Plato's philosophical writings that have survived include 25 dialogues as well as 13 letters – although their authenticity is at the moment in dispute. The dialogues generally feature Socrates as the main character, who constantly talks about things that their author, Plato, has more or less told him to say. Socrates uses a special method that combines *irony* and *dialectics*.

This method ensures that knowledge is not presented as a *fait accompli*, but must first be worked out, i.e. thought through. Thinking is seen as the art of 'synopsis'. In principle, it goes beyond the surface to point towards an essential quality that gives us a firm hold on real phenomena. This search for 'essential knowledge' accords well with 'the theory of ideas' that lies at the heart of Plato's philosophy. We should understand these ideas as the original images, or original forms, of real phenomena. They constitute a domain of their own, which is not of this world, although – willy nilly – it remains linked to that world, for otherwise there would be no reality, no knowledge in any form that was accessible to us. Human knowledge can function only because – like a continuous memory – it still participates in the realm of ideas. Thus, thanks to the mysterious resonance of these ideas, we always know more than we actually think we know. We look longingly at the vast realm of ideas, without needing to be directly conscious of it.

Like things on earth, these ideas are of different value – the highest ideas are the concepts of 'beauty and goodness'. From them, the immortal soul of human beings is derived. Before it entered the physical world and took on material form, the soul knew the world of ideas very intimately, and it is thus the soul that recaptures memories. To lead a life that accords with these ideas is to strive after the highest aims and to perfect one's knowledge to the best of one's ability.

The motivating force for such an undertaking is *eros*. This force has little to do with earthly love, but a great deal to do with love of what is everlasting. Anyone who follows eros will be leading a virtuous life, which also includes the harmony between personal happiness and sensible orderliness.

The virtues, including justice, wisdom, valour and presence of mind, create the bridge from knowledge and individuality to the state, which is supported by various social groups according to their virtues. It will come as no surprise to learn that the most important of these groups is made up of philosophers. They embody wisdom which, far from falling into anyone's lap, must be acquired through a long process of education.

Educated to rule, philosophers need people to do the donkey work of life. Among them are craftspeople and farmers, who need to provide for society's material well-being; warriors, who must be ready immediately to defend the state; and, last but not least, the slaves, who are responsible for the hard labour.

Why Plato made philosophers into rulers – on paper, at least – can apparently be explained by his own act of defiance. Rather than feeling contradicted by the Sicilian episode, Plato seems to have felt affirmed. This feeling must come from the innate superiority of philosophy, which, as everyone knows, can turn practice into theory. Imagining philosophers as rulers is a bold concept, which is open to ridicule. And in this context, we should not forget that no philosopher subsequently came forward who was willing to live in the kind of philosopher-state that Plato envisaged.

Such a state would probably be ruled with more austerity than wisdom. And let us not forget that neither Plato nor his philosophy are known for their jocularity. As he himself wrote: 'It is unseemly to be too inclined to laughter' – a view he always held.

While Plato's political philosophy has often been ridiculed –

not entirely unfairly – his 'theory of ideas or forms' has effortlessly stood the test of time. The theory argued the case for enduring memories, in which everyone can share. Its certainty is echoed in human beings' everlasting longing that something – perhaps even everything – once considered of value can go on existing for ever. Even a convinced realist can have the necessary insight – 'like a flash of light, suddenly struck in the soul by an escaping spark of fire, finds its own nourishment in itself'.

Plato the poet, who was always the equal of Plato the philosopher, could have added something else, as if by way of temporary consolation – a memory of the end that was not a final end. As his verse says: 'You were a morning star once, shining down for the living;/now in death you light the way for the dead as an evening star.'

'The life of Socrates is mainly known to us through the writings of Plato, who was one of his pupils and who became one of the greatest philosophers of all time . . .'
SW 55

Plotinus

In the third century AD, during which the dominant Roman Empire had been responsible for a catalogue of crisis and disintegration, the Greek spirit, which seemed to have disappeared entirely, came to be honoured afresh.

In *Hellenism*, this spirit enjoyed a new flowering, and *Plato* was celebrated as the first and best of all the Hellenes. The philosophy pursued by his admiring followers was later called Neoplatonism. The leading Neoplatonist was Plotinus (*c.*204–70). Reputedly, he was always so highly intellectual that he felt ashamed – and sometimes even forgot – to 'be a body'. Plotinus spent his most successful years in Rome, where he taught from 244 onwards, and where he was surrounded by a devoted circle of followers.

His philosophy makes Plato's world of ideas even more spiritual, taking them further upwards into the heavens. Up high, in a graduated cosmos, goodness resides, in the form of the 'All-One', which is so good that human reason cannot readily comprehend it. Only a process of 'procession' or transition, what Plotinus also calls 'emanation' or 'renunciation', which allows the All-One to flow into the 'world-intellect', can ensure sufficient access for perception to be possible.

In its turn, the world-intellect or world-spirit is a constituent part of the 'world-soul', which is made up of many individual souls, and which contains the world of ideas within it. As in Plato's philosophy, this world of ideas is the real centre of truth.

At the lower end of this spiritual step-ladder, we find 'matter', which Plotinus does not regard very highly. For him it represents 'evil', the eternal adversary of goodness. As ever, the goal of all knowledge remains the 'ecstatic' – the perfectly internalized realization of the 'One'. Thus anyone who has risen high enough can reach this state by climbing up the step-ladder of the 'real spirit' and achieving the *unio mystica* (see *Mysticism*) – which is the same thing as happiness.

'Plotinus believed that the world is a span between two poles . . .'
SW 113

Politics

· ·

The term comes from the Greek phrase, *ta politika*, the business of the state, and originally meant the entire science of life in state and community. This kind of life was highly admired – it was meant to be a 'good life', aiming at more than the development of an individual self.

Nowadays, as we hardly need telling, politics has largely detached itself from norms and moral convictions, even though these continue to be well regarded and to feature in fine speeches. According to one saying, politics is 'nothing but a trade', though it is hard to see what this particular trade is trying to sell. Politicians, the practitioners of politics, are constantly engaged in trying to convince someone of something – a difficult task when they are continually exposed to carping criticism.

'Politics . . . He {Aristotle} says that man is by nature a "political animal" . . .'
SW 97

Protagoras

Protagoras (*c.*485–*c.*415 BC) was probably the first philosopher to claim the profession of 'Sophist', which in his day was still considered something positive. The Sophists – from the Greek *sophistes*, meaning 'master' or 'artist' – were itinerant teachers of virtue and oratory, whose negative image dates from the time they appeared in the philosophy of *Socrates* and *Plato*. There, they are considered too pedantic, with a liking for intellectual nit-picking.

That said, according to other accounts, Protagoras, the most famous Sophist, was a highly honorable and intelligent person. His philosophy advocated a form of relativism which demands that human beings find their own standards of thought and behaviour. No one, Protagoras believed, can help them achieve these – not even the gods, of whom he says: 'As regards the gods, I cannot tell whether they exist or do not exist, nor what form they take; for much stands in the way of such knowledge: both the obscurity of the matter and the brevity of human life.'

Thus, although his truths are relative and home-made, Protagoras lays great stress on social coherence. A good state with a good sense of community is a value in itself, and this should not be arbitrarily called into question.

'"Man is the measure of all things," said the Sophist *Protagoras* . . .'
SW 54

Rationalism

Rationalism emphasizes the role of the *ratio*, the Latin word for *reason*, to which it entrusts a lot and – even more importantly – from which it expects a great deal.

Rationalism often used to follow the exact patterns of mathematical science. As such, it was especially popular in the Age of *Enlightenment*. Among other places, we find it in the philosophies of *Descartes*, *Spinoza* and *Leibniz*.

The ideal of rationalist knowledge was characterized by positive excess – everything can be known if only one is prepared to search thoroughly and intelligently enough. Nowadays, however, at a time when people seem to know more than ever before, there are hardly any rationalists left.

'Like every aspect of Plato's philosophy, his political philosophy is characterized by *rationalism* . . .'
SW 77–8

John Rawls

The American philosopher John Rawls (born 1921) was influenced by the practical philosophy of *Kant*. While initially seeing the concept of 'justice' for what it is – 'justice as fairness' – he distinguishes it from an individual's personal requirements, which will only (re)gain importance when society's members organize it along fundamentally altruistic lines.

John Rawls believes that there are rights whose validity extends beyond all social demands. As he wrote: 'Each person possesses an inviolability founded on justice that even the welfare of society as a whole cannot override . . . Therefore in a just society . . . the rights secured by justice are not subject to political bargaining or to the calculus of social interests.'

'A moral philosopher called John Rawls attempted to say something about it with the following example . . .'
SW 334

(Quotation from: *A Theory of Justice*, by John Rawls, OUP, 1972 and 1973, pp. 3–4)

Reason

· ·

People have always thought other people capable of a great deal – not just bad things, but also love, sympathy, hatred and reason. People like to think they are rational, and often imagine others sadly lacking in this respect. Reason is a human being's ability to grasp and evaluate wider interrelations beyond the normal range of understanding, while maintaining a certain objectivity.

According to *Kant*, who was arguably the most rational of all philosophers, reason is 'the very highest faculty of perception'. Although he was very fond of reason, Kant also recognized its limitations. When faced with anything that surpasses the immediate limits of human experience, reason can only speculate – however brilliantly – about God, the soul, the beginning and end of the world, death and an afterlife.

The questions arising from these speculations repeatedly challenge human reason. Kant himself says: 'As regards perception, human reason is faced with a special dilemma: on the one hand, it is constantly assailed by questions which it cannot dismiss, for they arise from the very nature of reason itself; on the other hand, it cannot answer them either, as they go beyond any power of human reason.'

Other philosophers have been less restrained in their attitude to reason. *Hegel*, for example, made reason, which is also mind or spirit, into a world-principle. *Fichte*, for his part, declared that reason strives 'towards omnipotence' and is, accordingly, the 'ultimate purpose' of our lives on earth. This attitude also led back to philosophy's beginnings. Even by the time of early Greek philosophy – that of, say, *Anaxagoras* – reason had acquired creative and organizational qualities that go beyond individual capacities. Thereafter, in the *Stoa*, for instance, it became the reason of the world, which can be equated with God.

Nowadays, people obviously treat the idea of reason with considerable caution. In our lives, we concentrate on change, avoiding boredom, even stasis – anything not to be rational. In *Goethe*'s *Faust*, Mephistopheles is presumably right to make the value of reason dependent on who is taking advantage of it. As he says: Reason becomes nonsense, comfort, torment/God help you if you're a child of reason!'

'In the same way, everybody can grasp philosophical truths if they just use their innate reason . . .'
SW 56

Renaissance

··

The word means literally 'rebirth', and it expresses the atmosphere of a new start. In reality, it meant the re-enlivening of classical ideas and – allied with that – the rediscovery of human beings as creatures in their own right, no longer prepared to skulk away as predestined sinners.

The zenith of the Renaissance, which produced *chefs d'oeuvre* primarily in the fine arts, took place in the fifteenth century, and its favourite sites were Italy and France. By the late sixteenth century, it had died back. While material hardships also played their part, the atmosphere of a new start was at an end, and people were once again faced with their usual anxieties.

'The Renaissance . . . O divine lineage in mortal guise . . .'
SW 157

Romanticism

Romanticism was born once people had decided that the *Enlightenment* had been enlightening enough. Was there not – people then began to ask – something beyond worthy *rational* insights? The mysteries of the ego, for example, or the treasures of the real world – including their darker, more hidden sides – as well as emotional yearnings and the splendours of *nature*, which may reveal more about God and his heavens than obligatory church attendance.

Literary Romanticism, which preceded philosophical Romanticism, also had more to offer than the latter. It attempted to embrace the raw vitality of life – including the life of ordinary people, which until then intellectuals had found amusing rather than inspiring. Before long, philosophical Romanticism tried to build this new-found vitality – as well as a suitably strong sense of personal identity – into its system.

The philosopher and writer *Novalis* sketched out a truly Romantic view of life: 'Insofar as I give something everyday a sublime meaning, or an ordinary object an enigmatic appearance, insofar as I endow something familiar with the dignity of unfamiliarity, or make something finite appear infinite – then I am rendering it Romantic . . .'

And from Novalis's fellow-writer, Achim von Arnim, comes the following exquisite description of a Romantic's delight in living. 'Anyone who has ever lost and forgotten themselves when dancing, anyone who has watched a balloon quietly drift up into the air like the sun, has left earth-bound mortality behind . . . anyone who has ever . . . seen a whole armada weighing anchor in the sunshine, when it has taken only a few moments – full of hustle and bustle on masts and spars – for these castles and galleries, as golden as the scales on a fish, to float calmly out of sight in the sea that is bordered by air – all things which surround us and which we encounter – must believe in a higher expression of life, in a higher form of art, than the one which surrounds us and which we encounter, on a Sunday after a working week, to which everyone is sensitive . . .'

'Romanticism . . . the path of mystery leads inwards . . .'
SW 284

Jean-Jacques Rousseau

Rousseau (1712–78), who was also a musician, deliberately chose to be a philosopher. He came from a poor background and started working as a copper-engraver. While still a young man, he found a rich woman patron, who also became his lover and gave him the opportunity for private studies, through which he continued his education.

Later on, he developed into a 'self-made man' of knowledge, who was prickly when criticized. He achieved his breakthrough into philosophy when he entered a contest organized by the Academy of Dijon. He answered the competition question: 'Has the reintroduction of arts and sciences contributed to purifying morals?' with an essay that won first prize, even though it contradicted prevailing optimism about progress.

Human beings, Rousseau's argument ran, have distanced themselves from an originally good 'state of nature' and have become 'self-seeking'. In giving their personal welfare and 'private property' prominence over the communal good, they think they are expressing their individual freedom.

Winning the Dijon competition made Rousseau famous overnight. He now entered his most productive phase, writing several books and finding himself in the public gaze. Nor did Rousseau content himself with a negative diagnosis of social issues. As the state of nature he so admired could not be recreated, he hoped to see human beings establish a community in which, by means of a 'social contract', they would achieve a 'general will' to the benefit of everyone.

It is not only as a philosopher that Rousseau is a controversial figure, but also as an educationalist. *Emile*, his novel of inner development, was a rhapsody on the virtues of loving, scrupulous education, which became a best-seller. That said, it was maliciously compared with Rousseau's own conduct as a father. As soon as his five children were born, Rousseau had packed them all off to the foundling hospital.

During his final years, Rousseau fell victim to a kind of paranoia. Imagining enemies everywhere, he thought that his friends had betrayed him and that his patrons had sold him down the river. The 'most illustrious thinker in Europe', as the Press had described him, died an embittered man. On one of his last sheets of manuscript he scribbled the words: 'From human beings I expect nothing but insults, lies and betrayal. Eternal Providence, my hopes reside in you . . .'

'Rousseau proposed the catchphrase "We should return to nature" . . .'
SW 262

Bertrand Russell

Russell (1872–1970) was highly honoured during his lifetime, winning the Nobel Prize for Literature in 1950, as well as arousing a great deal of controversy. He was active as a mathematician, philosopher and writer, and he was also a pugnacious pacifist and social critic.

As a radical democrat, Russell made few friends. People were more inclined to allow him to be the kind of philosopher who brought the *empiricism* of his countrymen, *Locke* and *Hume*, up to date. Russell himself described his philosophy as 'logical atomism'. He believed that reality can be divided up into very small 'constituents', and that these can be given 'logically proper names'. This demands something akin to an 'ideal language', which must develop in a special way in order to be readily understood.

In justifying his laudable but sometimes rather frenetic commitment to peace on earth, Russell claimed to be motivated by 'three passions'. He believed that the 'good life' is 'one inspired by love and guided by knowledge'. His third passion, a feeling for suffering human beings, he once expressed thus: 'I think we can, however imperfectly, mirror the world, like Leibniz's monads; and I think it is the duty of a philosopher to make himself as undistorting a mirror as he can.'

'An empiricist of our own century, Bertrand Russell, has provided a more grotesque example . . .'
SW 231

Jean-Paul Sartre

Sartre (1905–80) was a teacher, writer and philosopher. Together with his lifelong partner, *Simone de Beauvoir*, he developed a philosophy of 'freedom', which takes all its defining qualities from an individual's existence.

Originally, human beings are free, their freedom residing in their capacity for 'transcendence'. They have power over themselves and their situation, which they can go beyond, transform and, at the same time, refashion in their own sensibilities. Accordingly, people do not act only in isolation, but also discover their social role. In reality, they are not alone, but are affected by the 'Other's gaze'. At first, this appears to restrict human freedom, but in fact it reinforces it. In other words, the Other's gaze, which temporarily makes the subject into an object, is returned, leading to a process of *dialectical* exchange, or mutual recognition.

Sartre helped *existentialism* regain a certain status. He himself did not think labels important, and he thought that the existence of human beings, who, after all, live in terms of 'a fundamental state of freedom', had been misinterpreted. The range of 'choice' open to human beings is not just a one-off option, but a lifelong process of decision making, which needs to be renewed every day. In a way, therefore, human beings are 'condemned' to be free. Sartre argued that they sometimes feel they are 'carrying the burden of the whole world on their shoulders' because they are 'responsible for the world and for themselves as living creatures'.

Sartre always took pleasure in keeping his own existence flexible. He did not hesitate to call intellectual views into question or suddenly to subjugate his own philosophy to that of another thinker. This happened, for example, when he declared himself a *Marx*ist. While irritating some of his own followers, this upset orthodox Marxists even more, as they did not believe that Sartre had completely converted from his philosophy of freedom.

Nothing daunted, Sartre himself embraced an outlook that is no longer very fashionable, even though its ideas are undoubtedly better than the discredited systems that until recently drew on them. As Sartre put it: 'Far from being exhausted, Marxism is still in its first youth . . . it has only just started to develop. It remains the philosophy of our age; it cannot be rendered obsolete because the conditions which engendered it have yet to be transcended . . .'

'Sartre said that "existentialism is humanism" . . .'
SW 378

Scepticism

··

Within philosophy, scepticism is akin to a stable currency. In other words, the doubt that all true sceptics have up their sleeves can be applied to anything. Accordingly, it should come as no surprise that, as a trend in philosophy, scepticism has survived without any difficulty.

Michel de Montaigne (1533–92) was a great sceptic. He wrote: 'We are taught to live only when life is over. A hundred students will have caught syphilis before they get to the chapter in Aristotle on moderation.' Elsewhere, he said: 'The world is made up of chatter, and I have never met anyone who did not say too much rather than too little; even so, we devote half our lives to it.'

'When it came to acquiring certain knowledge, many of his {Descartes'} contemporaries voiced a total philosophical *skepticism* . . .'
SW 195

Friedrich Wilhelm Joseph Schelling

Schelling (1775–1854) first drew attention to himself as a youth of exceptional brilliance, but as time went on and the young genius grew up, he was heavily criticized. Schelling also had to watch *Hegel*, his fellow-student from Tübingen, overtake him in terms of renown – something he never expected him to achieve. This made him hypersensitive, and he became rather paranoid. In his philosophy, the circumstances of Schelling's life are reflected in a development from his light, open, generally optimistic early work to the often inaccessible philosophy of his old age.

After completing his studies, Schelling initially took up a post – as was then the custom – as a private tutor. Shortly thereafter, however, and at an early age, he was appointed a professor in Jena. Here, he moved among the leading lights of German *Romanticism*. Subsequent professorships followed in Würzburg, Munich and Erlangen. In 1841 he was summoned to Berlin, ostensibly to 'uproot the dragon-teeth of Hegelianism that had been sown there'.

If this aim ever existed, Schelling failed miserably to fulfil it. Remembering his early renown, students at first flocked to Schelling's lectures. Before long, however, he had annoyed his audience with a 'monotonous, interminable, largely incomprehensible lecture', and not long afterwards he found himself addressing rows of mainly empty benches. In 1846 he retired, hurt, from academic duties, and thereafter continued his studies only in private.

Within the philosophy of German *idealism*, Schelling played the role of a philosopher of *nature*, though he felt understretched in this capacity. Schelling accorded nature an independence that his colleagues, *Fichte* and *Hegel*, had failed to grant her. Schelling established a link between nature and mind or spirit, by means of 'absolute rationality'. He was seeking to answer the question of how nature and mind not only exist side by side, but also influence and interpenetrate one another; or, as he himself expressed it, how the 'course of nature . . . can exist outside us' and, at the same time 'find the way to our mind'.

As an idealist, Schelling criticizes the kind of idealism that refuses to acknowledge its own origins and which therefore becomes 'itself unreal' and 'something which needs to be explained'. In his early philosophy, 'art' also played a special role. Along with 'imagination', art is the consoling third force that is able to unite nature and freedom.

In later years, he did not have full confidence in this outline of a system. He indulged in complicated deliberations revolving around the 'interaction' between *reason* and *freedom*, a two-way process that he regarded more sceptically than his predecessors.

Schelling believed that reality, which has for a long time failed to exist – or, at least, has failed to be fashioned in a rational form – retains a small element that is immune to philosophical interpretation. True reality, he felt, is – and must surely remain – 'more potent' than the concept that tries to encapsulate it.

Even though it may sound a little hermetic, Schelling's late philosophy still offers some unusual ideas. One idea is what Schelling calls the 'ray of light', which allows nature to open her eyes within a human being and thus to become aware that 'she is there'.

'Schelling saw a "world spirit" in nature, but he saw the same "world spirit" in the human mind . . .'
SW 291

Friedrich Schiller

Schiller (1759–1805) admired *Kant* so greatly that he felt he had to improve him. The writer was particularly dissatisfied with Kant's 'moral law', which, in his opinion, laid too much emphasis on 'duty' and not enough on 'inclination'. Schiller believed that people should feel inclined to behave morally. In this way, a sense of duty can take on a human quality.

One of Schiller's most fascinating ideas concerns human beings' 'impulse to play'. As he himself wrote: 'People can only take seriously what is agreeable, what is good, what is perfect; with beauty, on the other hand, people can play . . . In other words, not to put too fine a point on it, human beings play only when they are, in the fullest sense, human, and they are only fully human when they are at play.'

Shortly afterwards, Schiller withdrew from philosophy and went back to writing. He did this out of firm conviction: 'This much is now clear, that the poet is the only true human being, and compared to a poet, the best philosopher is merely a caricature.'

'The German poet *Schiller* developed Kant's thought further . . .'
SW 288

Seneca

....

Everything is possible in philosophy – even, or perhaps, especially – the ability to hold diametrically opposed opinions at the same time. The view that human beings were sacred to other human beings was later turned into *Hobbes*'s view that human beings behaved like wolves to other human beings. At all events, whenever three philosophers meet and take at least four different views, only the fifth or sixth of these can be correct.

Seneca (*c.*4 BC–AD 65) is another example of what befalls philosophers – *Marcus Aurelius* being a case in point – who move in political circles, which is generally an unhappy experience. Seneca held a number of high offices and tutored the nefarious Nero, a thoroughly thankless task, which reached a fitting end. The Emperor compelled his erstwhile tutor to take his own life, which Seneca duly did – though if the roles had been reversed, the former pupil would scarcely have responded so obediently to a similar instruction.

As a philosopher, Seneca followed the *Stoic* pattern. He believed in a more or less sovereign *reason*, and considered it necessary – if only to maintain a well-organized community – that human beings should hold their passions and emotions in check. Seneca wrote the splendid sentence: 'One can leap into the sky even from a dismal corner.'

'Some years later, the Stoic *Seneca* . . . said that "to mankind, mankind is holy" . . .'
SW 111

Socrates

The fact that Socrates (470–399 BC) was such an enigma has kept his memory alive in the history of philosophy. As a historical figure, he was largely created by *Plato*, who ensured that his teacher was remembered long after his death. From then on, a picture has emerged of him that we can easily recognize – Socrates the passionate advocate of wisdom and also a trouble-maker. We see him as someone strolling about the squares and streets of Athens, with, it appears, nothing better to do than involve people in conversations, which generally begin inno-cently, but then gather pace and gain profundity. The technique of pursuing philosophy as a practical conversational art, focus-ing on the matter in hand and usually paying scant regard to the speaker, has become a model for others to follow. People have greatly valued this 'Socratic method', probably aware that the technique has – or rather, had – a great deal to offer, even though it is not practicable everywhere.

What do we know about the historical Socrates? He was the son of a sculptor and a midwife, which could also be taken symbolically, for Socrates liked to talk metaphorically, and believed that philosophy should follow so called maieutics, the 'art of midwifery', which consists of persuading people to part with knowledge that they are not aware they have.

For a while, he himself worked as a sculptor and stonemason. He then married the famous – or infamous – Xanthippe. She was exceedingly quarrelsome, and was at least as ugly as he apparently was. A wiser man since his experiences with Xanthippe, his answer to any prospective bridegroom who asked his advice was as follows: 'Whatever you do, you'll regret it!' That said, Socrates probably owes his conversion to philo-sophy to Xanthippe. When she threw him out of their house, he had little choice but to turn to philosophy.

Before that, however, he was a soldier in the Peloponnesian War, in which he apparently showed great bravery. However, some contemporary witnesses report that even on the battlefield he was noticeable for his 'odd behaviour'. Upon returning to

Athens, he worked as a councillor and soon began to make enemies. As people in power saw it, he had a talent for mischief making.

They also disapproved of his way of life. They did not like to see him mixing with people and philosophizing with them, especially as they were afraid he might go spreading some damaging opinions. Finally, he was accused of impiety, as well as corrupting young people. Some of the patrons who stayed true to him tried to build a bridge for Socrates, who could have gone into exile and thus avoided the death penalty.

Yet the philosopher dug his heels in. He was not aware of having committed any crime and, as is well known, spoke eloquently to the court in his own defence. In this speech, he said: 'For as long as I'm still breathing and am still capable of it, I shall never cease to philosophize, admonishing you and unmasking you, whichever one of you I happen to come across, and I'll go on saying the same as I have always said . . .' He also said: 'We need not take any notice whatever of what the vast crowd may say about us – only of what one person says to us, the one who understands right and wrong – the One who is truth incarnate.'

In the final analysis, people were convinced that the philosopher had almost provoked the authorities into taking legal steps against him – and thus deserved punishment. Socrates was condemned to death. He took the cup of poison and asked his friends to leave. His last words were reputedly these: 'Now it is time – for me to die, and for you to live. Which of us is going to the better place is known to no one – except God.'

'Socrates . . . is possibly the most enigmatic figure in the entire history of philosophy . . .'
SW 55

Baruch Spinoza

He led a quiet and retiring life, he never trod on anyone's toes, and yet he was vilified more than most other philosophers. He was called a 'blaspheming Jew', a 'despicable monster', a 'foreign animal', a 'lunatic and a ghastly little devil'. His everyday life cannot have been the reason for these insults. Nor can his philosophy, though that is what put people's backs up.

Spinoza (1632–77) spent most of his life in Amsterdam, and earned his living there as a lens-grinder. He died of tuberculosis in great poverty. Even as a young man, he came into conflict with his local Jewish community. He reputedly described the Old Testament as the 'most contradictory of all works'. He was summarily dismissed from his community, which only reinforced his natural inclination to stand alone.

His first book, which appeared under a pseudonym and was swiftly banned, also failed to win him any friends. In it, he demanded freedom of thought, which he saw not only as something of value in itself, but also as 'useful', in that it 'prevents human beings from saying, day after day, something other than what they think'.

Spinoza's philosophy is God-fearing, and this makes it all the more astonishing that he could call down so many insults upon his head. What probably angered Spinoza's contemporaries most was his view of God. He makes him into an all-embracing *substance*, comprising the world, objects and human beings, who are only 'ways of being', or 'modi' of this one and only substance.

Spinoza himself wrote the following: 'I hold an opinion about God and nature which is vastly different from the view which recent Christians are in the habit of defending. For I consider God to be the innate cause of all things, though not the cause that overrides everything. What I say is that everything is in God and set in motion by God.'

According to Spinoza, God reveals himself in the rich variety of his Creation, from which he has never withdrawn. This is a fascinating idea, though it also has its less agreeable sides, as a contemporary critic of Spinoza's found. He wrote: 'All the insane and repulsive ideas people have, the blasphemies and terrifying chimeras of human reason, which is forever chattering away about nothing – are all these horrors supposed to be the thoughts and designs of God, through which he depicts and reflects himself . . . Are we really expected to believe that?'

'Spinoza . . . God is not a puppeteer . . .'
SW 205

Josef Stalin

Stalin (1879–1953), whose real name was Dzhugashvili, illustrates the fact that dictators do not necessarily have to behave monstrously in order to terrify the life out of people. The leader of Soviet Russia who succeeded *Lenin* liked to appear jovial. He was an exceptionally homely man, who, when evening came, sang lovely sad songs, and on certain occasions – like his colleague, Hitler – enjoyed dandling small children on his knee.

That said, his approach to people who didn't suit his purposes was not to beat about the bush – just to eliminate them. Stalin's colossal sang-froid stemmed from his knowledge of what holds the world together and makes it revolve. He saw himself not only as the father of his subjects, but also as a disinterested advocate of philosophy. For him, this consisted mostly of Marxism-Leninism, whose message he helped spread with significant works of his own.

He specialized in philology. When in 1950 the philological experts speculated for too long on whether or not language formed part of the philosophical 'superstructure' of society, Stalin pronounced authoritatively on the issue. He wrote in his newspaper, *Pravda* (*The Truth*): 'Is it correct to say that language is a superstructure above the foundation of society? No, that is not correct . . .' Then Stalin gave his interpretation: 'Language is not created by one particular society or another, but by the whole course of the history of society.'

'In our own century, Lenin, Stalin, Mao and many others also made their contribution to Marxism, or Marxism-Leninism . . .'
SW 326

Henrik Steffens

This Norwegian philosopher got on well with the Germans, especially their so-called *Romantics*. He knew them all and wrote some intelligent reviews of their works. Occasionally, he also made some sensitive interpretations, in which both texts and authors yielded remarkable revelations about themselves.

Steffens (1773–1845) was a professor in Halle, Breslau and Berlin. His own philosophy pursues the discrepancy between the world as a whole entity and individuality. Human beings have lived out this contradiction through the whole history of their development – and must go on enduring it. As the only form of thinking with 'a full overview', philosophy might – so Steffens argues – be the only science that can promote unity, even though this will not last for ever.

'The Norwegian-born naturalist *Henrik Steffens* . . . went to Copenhagen in 1801 to lecture on German Romanticism . . .'
SW 291

Stoa

. . . .

This philosophy, which was founded by the philosopher Zeno of Citium around 300 BC, derives its name from the place where it was taught, under the 'Stoa poikile', or 'painted portico', in Athens. The Stoa was a widespread philosophical tendency in ancient Greece. Then, in imperial Rome, thanks to prominent Stoics such as *Seneca* and *Marcus Aurelius*, it temporarily achieved a kind of modishness as a philosophy.

The Stoa was liberal enough to assimilate ideas from other attitudes to life, which it then applied to its own pattern of thought. Central to Stoic philosophy is the notion of a power that is interwoven with the cosmos and also controls it. It is simultaneously God and *nature*, as well as the 'world-soul' and 'world-*reason*'. Human beings play a part in this power. They belong to it, but as individuals they can only make a modest contribution to the great events of the world, which follow a pattern of creation and decay dictated by the laws of necessity.

That said, the Stoics believed in a kind of free will, which they cloaked in a cunning demand – live freely but in accordance with nature. Stoic *ethics* emphasizes moderation, which also helps to strike a balance between the individual's inevitable self-interest and the overarching good of the community.

'The name "Stoic" comes from the Greek word for portico (*stoa*) . . .'
SW 110

Substance

··

This term comes from the Latin word *substantia*, and it means what is self-sufficient, enduring or fundamental. A substance is like a rock braving the breakers of phenomena. That said, we need to make an effort to work out what a substance is and what it is not.

The philosopher *Descartes* opted for two substances: thought and matter. For his colleague, *Spinoza*, this was one substance too many. For him, the only substance worth the name was 'what is innate in itself and understood as such', namely God, who is at the same time *nature* and everything else. *Kant* also thought hard about substance, of which he wrote: 'No matter how radically phenomena may change, substance remains constant, and its quantity in nature neither increases nor diminishes.'

Today – in philosophy, at least, – the term is no longer very up to date. Frequently, when the word comes up, people understand 'substance' in an intellectual sense. This is why political speeches are often thought to lack what is called 'substance'. By the same token, one might feel 'substantially' affected when one has to listen to too many of these speeches.

'One substance is *thought*, or the "mind," the other is *extension*, or matter . . .'
SW 200

Surrealism

Surrealism set great store by 'subrealism', or what *Freud* called the subconscious. The Surrealists held this to be more important than *consciousness*. Dreams, which had earlier served *Romanticism* as means of acquiring knowledge, took on a new significance.

Novalis, the poet-philosopher, whom Surrealists such as Bergson and Breton greatly admired, demonstrated at an early date how 'surrealistic' nascent certainties could be. He was visited by visions emanating from the grave of his dead beloved, Sophie – visions as real as the flow of thoughts that inspired them. As Novalis wrote: 'The weather darkened – first a squall, then lowering clouds, and finally a storm; all very sensual. That evening, I went to see Sophie. I was indescribably happy there. Moments of ecstatic enthusiasm. I sighed so deeply over her grave that the earth scattered before me like dust. Centuries sped by like instants.'

'The word surrealism comes from the French, and means "super realism". . .'
SW 366

Thales

. . . .

Sometimes, Thales (*c.*624–*c.*547 BC) is thought to mark the start of philosophical history. He was reputedly one of the first, if not the very first, to begin asking those awkward questions (see SW 12ff.) which philosophy is still asking. This is presumably because the answers still turn out to be so unsatisfactory.

Thales was also one of the first philosophers people made fun of. He was apparently very absent-minded, as well as scruffy and a bit strange – all of which means that he fulfilled the basic criteria of our cliché image of a philosopher. Nevertheless, Thales convinced sceptics by the results he achieved. He predicted the odd eclipse of the sun and – on request – he would also give weather forecasts. He was also a capable mathematician. He believed that the original substance and basic element of all life was water, which – according to him – even supported the earth.

There are several anecdotes about Thales. These not only are very funny, but also confirm how wise he was. Thus, when asked why he did not want to father any children, he reportedly made the classic response: 'For love of the children.'

'The first philosopher we know of is *Thales*, who came from Miletus, a Greek colony in Asia Minor . . .'
SW 28

Thucydides

Thucydides (c.460–c.399 BC) was not only a historian, but also commander-in-chief of a fleet that fought on the Athenian side in the Peloponnesian War between Athens and Sparta. His superiors accused him of cowardice in the face of the enemy, since he and his fleet merely watched passively while the colony of Amphipolis, which had been recommended to him as an ally, fell to the Spartans. Accordingly, Thucydides was banished, which left him plenty of time to write history.

As a historian, he was extremely concerned about factual accuracy. He had little time for supernatural explanations, conjectures about the gods' possible interventions in the course of history, or the didactic advice and anecdotes that his colleague Herodotus liked to include in his histories.

'The best known Greek historians were *Herodotus* . . . and *Thucydides* . . .'
SW 46

Voltaire

Although his real name was François-Marie Arouet, he called himself Voltaire and he was a writer, philosopher and man of the world. As a writer, he made a fortune, as a philosopher he annoyed the great and good of his day, and as a man of the world he was always keen on grabbing the headlines.

Voltaire (1694–1778) was also able to be witty, which did not endear him to all his contemporaries – not even all his fellow-writers. *Rousseau*, for instance, who had achieved great fame through his watchword: 'Back to nature!', was piqued at Voltaire's response to his book, *On the Origins of Inequality between People*. Voltaire wrote: 'No one has ever wasted so much intelligence as you have in your effort to make us all animals again. One really feels like crawling about on all fours when one reads your work. Speaking personally, I gave up that habit sixty years ago, and so it's impossible for me to go back to it now . . .'

Voltaire, who enjoyed spreading news of his many (imaginary?) illnesses, was vain. This may explain why he liked to exaggerate his 'deficient schooling', describing himself as a 'half-educated philosopher'. His attitude to life was sceptical, even though he considered human beings capable of making a little progress. That said, he regarded his colleague *Leibniz*'s theory – that God had created the best of all possible worlds – as ludicrous.

Instead, with typical irony, he addressed some of his own questions to God. These include: 'The philosophy of "Everything is for the best" presents the Creator of nature as a powerful, wicked king, who doesn't give a damn whether four or five thousand people perish, or whether the rest drag out their days in poverty and distress . . . This leads one to ask whether God is in one place beyond all other places, or in all places at once? Does he take a corporeal or spiritual form? And how is one to tell? . . . "Know thyself!" is excellent advice, but only God is in a position to implement it in practice . . .'

'The important names are *Montesquieu*, *Voltaire*, and *Rousseau*, but there were many, many others . . .'
SW 260

Xenophanes

A well-known encyclopaedia of the ancient world states that Xenophanes (*c.*570–*c.*475 BC) was 'not an original philosopher'. This is simply not true. Judging by everything we know about him, Xenophanes was a far-sighted thinker whose views seem astonishingly up to date nowadays.

He criticized the views of God devised by human beings. These, he thought, turn out to be all too human – in other words, rather absurd – and they are as different as one person is from another. In Xenophanes' view, however, God, who is 'the greatest entity among gods and men', is 'not like mortals in any way whatsoever, neither physically nor spiritually'. Human beings can know about God, but they cannot really perceive him. In fact, Xenophanes believed, people's perceptive faculties are altogether inadequate. They have to settle for speculations, pragmatic values and provisional certainties. In this context, Xenophanes quotes a statement that might have come from a respected theory of knowledge of our own day: 'Things ought to be believed insofar as they resemble the truth . . .'

This insight presupposes that knowledge does not remain valid for always, but can be corrected in the course of time – as a result of substantial improvements in knowledge. In his words: 'The gods have not imparted everything to human beings from the very start, but in time, as they search diligently, so they discover more.'

Xenophanes led a restless life of wanderings, mostly through Greek southern Italy, though this did not prevent him from growing extremely old. His income reputedly included fees from the lectures he held in rich people's houses. He was convinced that human beings would never really be sure of themselves. He even expressed this in an exquisite poem: 'No human being ever knew certain truth, nor ever will/About the gods or any of the things of which I speak./Even if one day someone proclaims the most perfect truth,/He could

not know it was: for everything is shot through with specula-
tion.'

'One exponent of this view {criticizing myths} was the philosopher Xeno-
phanes . . .'
SW 23

Zeno of Citium

Zeno (*c*.336–264 BC) came from Cyprus and was a merchant by profession. He reputedly took up philosophy by accident, after one of his boats capsized and he took lodgings with an Athens book-dealer, who was studying a philosophical work. Looking over his shoulder, Zeno began to read and apparently knew at once that he would himself start searching for the truth.

Otherwise, the founder of the *Stoa* is described as a rather strange figure. He was a haggard, lanky man, always dressed rather shabbily, who used to cock his head when thinking. Despite these external peculiarities, which his enemies found curious, people soon began to praise his acumen, and he kept attracting more and more followers.

Zeno set great store by *reason*. Reason, he believed, is interwoven with everything and structures everything with inner necessity, thus 'completing the true essence of human beings'. For Zeno, reason has its own *freedom*, which is, however, restricted by this same necessity: 'Human beings are free only if they are free within themselves and do nothing but what their reason selects.' Reason also tells people 'what to do and . . . what not to do'. Virtue is what Zeno calls the voice of reason, which expresses moral necessity in human beings. Virtue 'is something to strive after for its own sake' and 'is its own reward'.

Zeno, who preferred his own company to other people's, recommends civic thinking in his philosophy. He maintains that we are duty-bound to help achieve the common good. As he himself expresses it: 'By our natures we are disposed towards integration, union, amalgamation into a state . . . Virtuous human beings will not live in isolation; they are . . . made for active life.'

'The Cynics were instrumental in the development of the *Stoic* school of philosophy . . . Its founder was *Zeno* . . .'
SW 110